100
BLUES LESSONS

BY CHAD JOHNSON CHRIS KRINGEL

CONTENTS

Lessons 1–50 by Chris Kringel

Lessons 51–100 by Chad Johnson

LESSON #1: THE BLUES SCALE

Want to play the blues? Do you know how to create a bluesy sounding melody, solo, or line? One of the key elements when learning to play the blues is the blues scale. The sound of this scale is the basic building block expressed in melodies, solos, and bass lines of blues music. What makes the blues scale different is its use of "blue notes," which are the ♭3rd, ♭5th, and ♭7th degrees of the major scale. These flattened notes create tension and convey a somewhat melancholy atmosphere. The formula for the blues scale is: 1–♭3–4–♭5–5–♭7.

EXAMPLE 1

Here is the E blues scale, starting from the open E string:

EXAMPLE 2

Here's the blues scale in C. This fingering can be moved around the neck to create the blues scale in any key.

Here is another way to look at the moveable blues scale shape:

EXAMPLE 3

Let's expand the blues scale by playing it in several octaves. We'll start at the low E on the E string and make our way up to the high E on the G string. This is a great way to expand the fingering beyond one octave.

Melodic Ideas

When we talk about the history of the blues, we often speak of how the music was used to express the emotional turmoil felt by the people of that time period. The primary intention of the blues is to convey emotion and feeling through the music. Learning the scales and the theory behind blues music is a tool for helping you understand this musical expression. The following are some bass lines based on the blues scale. Play through them and then try to create your own lines.

EXAMPLE 4

EXAMPLE 5

EXAMPLE 6

C7 GROOVE

It's your turn to create some bass lines and perhaps do a little soloing using the C blues scale. This track is a groove over a C7 chord. See what you can come up with!

LESSON #2: THE 12-BAR BLUES

The 12-bar blues is the most common type of blues. The structure was built from workers singing in the fields, using a call-and-response exchange, which eventually evolved into what we today call a 12-bar blues. It provides a common pattern for musicians to play over and is familiar to many.

One Chorus

When you play the blues, you play a form called the "chorus." The chorus consists of 12 measures and is built from three separate sections, each four measures long. These three sections build a story and follow a lyrical and/or melodic idea. The first four measures set up a situation or describe a problem, the next four measures respond by repeating what was said or played, and the last four measures elaborate on or are an answer to the problem—a resolution if you will. If it's an instrumental song, the melodic phrases are four measures long, followed by a repeat with some slight embellishment, and finally, a completion or resolution. Here is how it looks on a musical staff:

EXAMPLE 1

Chord Placement

Each section uses dominant seventh chords built off the first, fourth, and fifth degrees of the major scale, referred to as the I, IV, and V chords. It is essential that you internalize the structure and "hear" the changes; that way, you can stop thinking and just play the blues. The following example shows the simplest chord changes of a traditional 12-bar blues in the key of G.

EXAMPLE 2

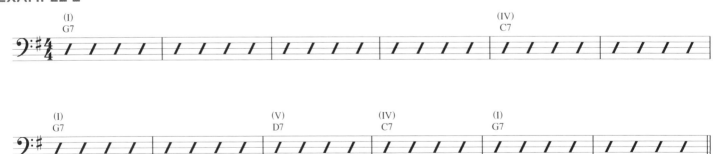

EXAMPLE 3

Now let's listen to and play along with an example. As I stated before, you'll want to internalize the sound of the chord changes until it becomes so natural that it's like breathing.

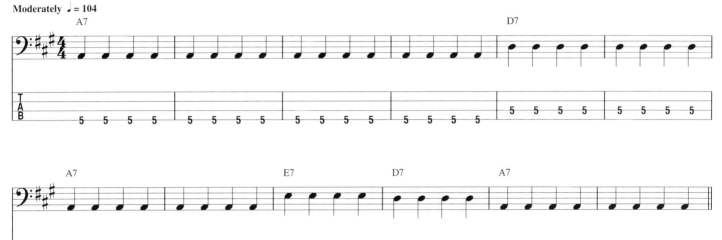

EXAMPLE 4

Another common harmony in a 12-bar blues is the V chord appearing in measure 12, right before the chorus repeats. This is as normal as playing the I chord here. In fact, the V chord is more commonly added. When in doubt, go to the V in the last measure!

There are several different tempos and grooves that can be used when playing the 12-bar blues, so listen to as many types as you can and become familiar with the various feels. That way, you will know what kind of groove to lay down in any situation.

LESSON #3: QUICK CHANGE

When someone on a gig says "standard 12-bar, quick change" or "this one is a 12-bar with a quick four," what they are telling you is that the second measure of the chorus jumps to the IV chord before moving back down to the I chord for measures 3–4. It's that simple! Let's take a look.

EXAMPLE 1

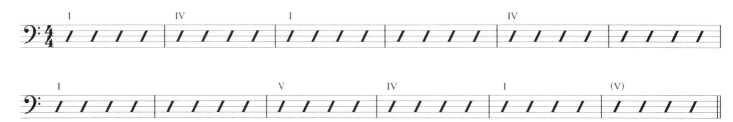

Sometimes, the "quick four" is only used during the solos of a 12-bar blues, not when the melody is being played. How will you know? Either someone will mention it or you'll have to hear it. Having a good ear—that is, being able to determine pitch changes—is an essential skill when playing the blues. Spending time listening to and playing along with blues recordings will help you develop your ear so you instantly notice when the quick four is upon you.

Quick Change Explorations

The best way to understand something is to spend time doing it. If it's fun for you, the process of learning will be more of a curious exploration, rather than a job that has to get done. The great thing about being a musician is that, in most cases, musicians love music. Therefore, learning by listening and playing becomes a fun way to pass time. Let's explore by playing several different 12-bar blues bass lines that follow the quick change, or quick four.

EXAMPLE 2

This one is a shuffle in the key of A.

EXAMPLE 3

Here's a country blues in G.

EXAMPLE 4

This example is a swing shuffle in B♭.

LESSON #4: THE SHUFFLE FEEL

When playing the blues, a feel that stands out above the rest is the shuffle. The shuffle feel consists of a triplet subdivision, which gives it a bouncy, skipping rhythm. This feel is the same as inserting a rest in the middle of an eighth-note triplet. Another way to look at a shuffle feel is to play the eighth notes in long-short fashion, rather than as equal values, tying the first two eighth notes of a triplet together and playing the third.

To keep things simple, a shuffle feel is notated with the following symbol at the top of a song. It spares the confusion of writing out so many triplets.

Playing the Shuffle

EXAMPLE 1

This example is a root-note shuffle feel. First, we will play it as a short shuffle, like an eighth-note triplet with a rest in between. Second, we will play it long, like a quarter note and eighth note in a triplet bracket. Each feel creates a different type of sound.

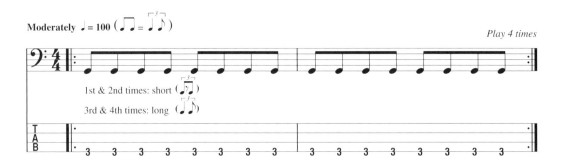

EXAMPLE 2

To get you familiar with the shuffle feel, here is a 12-bar blues in the key of E.

Swung Eighths

If you play two consecutive eighth notes so that the first eighth is played on the beat and the second eighth is played as if it were the third note of a triplet subdivision, the result is a shuffle feel. When the shuffle-feel symbol is present at the top of a song, the eighth notes should be swung. The only difference between the shuffle feel and the swing feel is that the shuffle is slightly more jagged and bouncy, whereas the swing feel is slightly smoother. Let's play a C blues scale pattern with straight eighth notes and then add a swing feel.

EXAMPLE 3

LESSON #5: TURNAROUNDS

The transition passage at the end of a blues form is called a turnaround. The turnaround is usually a two-bar progression that ends on the V chord, sonically adding a period to the end of a musical statement before taking you back (or "turning you around") to the top of the form.

Basic Turnarounds

The following examples are the last two bars of a 12-bar blues in the key of G.

TURNAROUND 1

This is one of the most commonly used turnarounds. Notice the "kick" on the upbeat of beat 2 of the last measure.

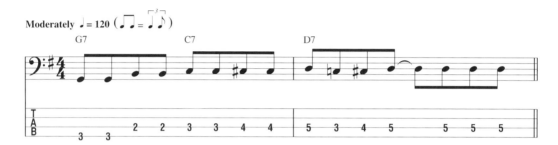

TURNAROUND 2

This is the same progression as Turnaround 1, but walks down instead.

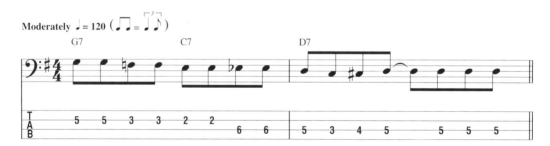

TURNAROUND 3

This turnaround stays on the V chord in bar 12 like the others, but uses a triplet to add momentum.

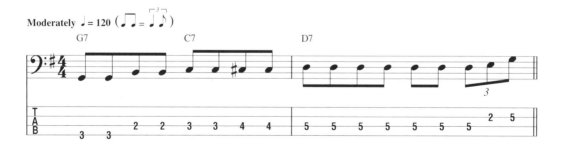

Turnarounds 4 and 5 are walking blues examples that use the same formula as before.

TURNAROUND 4

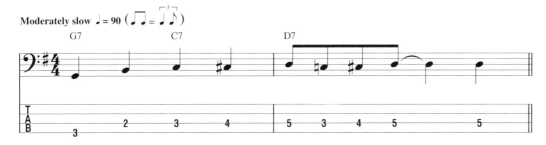

TURNAROUND 5

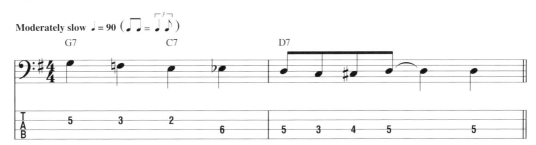

Another common turnaround, especially in jazz-blues progressions, is I–VI–ii–V. Below are two variations in the key of C.

TURNAROUND 6

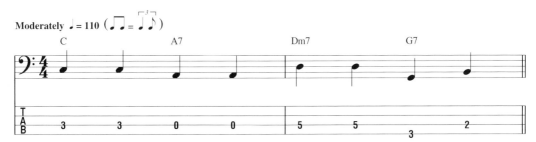

TURNAROUND 7

LESSON #6: INTROS

There are many ways to begin a 12-bar blues. The intro, or introduction, is a section of music placed in front of the form to set up the song. Usually, the intro is taken from the song form, most often the last four bars, starting on the V chord.

From the "Five"

INTRO 1

As the heading implies, this intro starts on the V chord, which is borrowed from the ninth measure of a 12-bar blues. Just remember: the last four bars of the song are typically used to set up the song. The following examples are intros that start "from the five." Here is a root-note shuffle in the key of A.

INTRO 2

Here's a boogie-line intro in the key of E.

INTRO 3

In this box-shape shuffle in the key of D, notice that the V (A7) chord is located in the lower octave relative to the I chord.

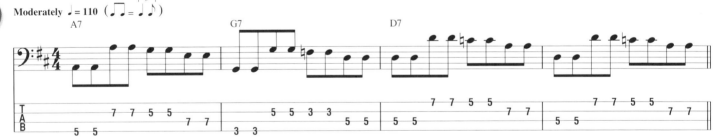

INTRO 4

Here is an intro for a 12/8 slow blues in the key of G. Notice the pickup notes that lead into the V chord, which is very common in a 12/8 slow blues intro.

On the "One"

On occasion, the band will vamp on the I chord until cued. All you need to do is play the correct feel until then. If you'd like, you can drop the V chord in before you go to the top of the song, to signal the beginning of the tune. Here is a rhumba in the key of G.

INTRO 5

From the "Four"

Sometimes an intro can be called from the IV chord, starting in measure 5 of a 12-bar blues. This is less typical but does happen on occasion. Here is a funky blues intro in the key of D.

INTRO 6

Tacet

Another common intro for the bassist is to not play at all; instead, entering at the top of the song. The best advice I can give is to listen and really "hear" the changes until they become instinctual. Spend time actively listening to recordings, look for open jams, and play with friends, because there is no practice that compares to the real experience of jumping in and playing the blues with others.

LESSON #7: ENDINGS

All good things must come to an end, but if the end is sloppy and chaotic, that is what the listener will remember. Nothing kills a song more than an ending that falls apart! In this lesson, we'll explore several standard endings.

ENDINGS 1A–B

Here is one of the most common endings in the blues genre, played over the last two bars of the form, along with a variation. This one's in the key of G. Hold that last note till you're cued!

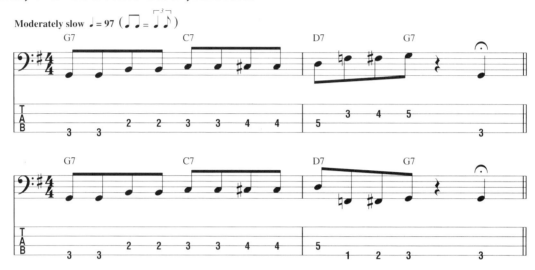

ENDINGS 2A–B

Here's the same ending (and a variation), except it descends from the I chord.

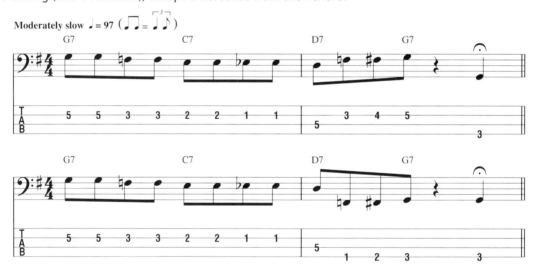

ENDINGS 3A–B

Another option is to alter one note in the last measure of the previous endings to make them sound more diatonic—and less chromatic.

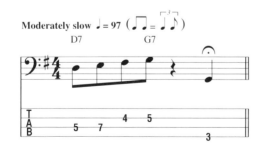

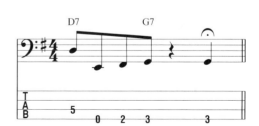

ENDINGS 4A–B

Another common ending incorporates a rhythmic "kick" on the "and" of beat 1 of measure 11 (measure 1 in the example). This one's in the key of A.

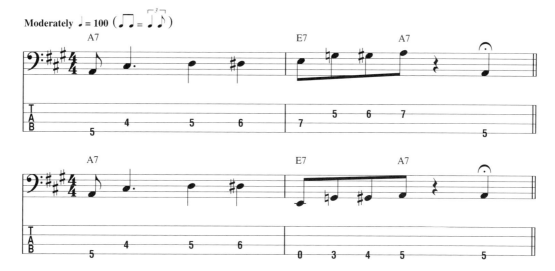

ENDINGS 5A–B

This ending (and its variation) is the descending version of the previous example.

ENDING 6

Here is an ending that incorporates half-step resolution to the I chord. This ending is often used in slower blues songs and is in the key of C.

ENDING 7

Another common ending, this one walks down the minor pentatonic scale—in this case, A minor pentatonic.

LESSON #8: THE "BUMP": THE ROOT SHUFFLE

Sometimes the best and most effective option is to play it simple, and the root shuffle is just that. The root shuffle consists of playing the root note for each chord change in a 12-bar blues, or "bumping" the root. This is a highly effective and hypnotic approach. Although it may seem simple, when playing for the sake of the groove, bumping the root is one of my favorite types of shuffles to play.

Walk Up or Walk Down

To create some movement in the progression, you can use a walk-up to the IV chord or you can just stay on the root until you get familiar with the sound that you want to hear. Another good note choice is the ♭7th while on the IV chord in measures 6 and 10, just before you go back to the I chord (i.e., beat 4). My best advice is to actively listen to blues recordings and play along and learn what sounds good, especially when exploring walk-ups and walk-downs.

EXAMPLE 1

Here is a slow, greasy root shuffle in the key of E.

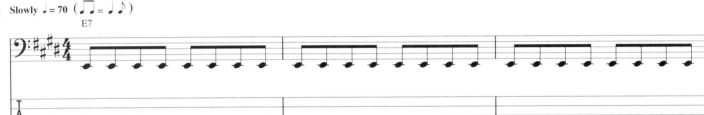

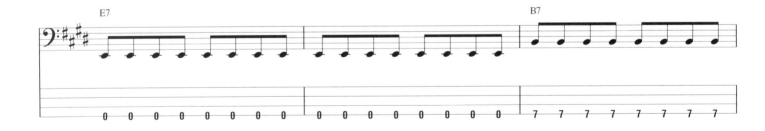
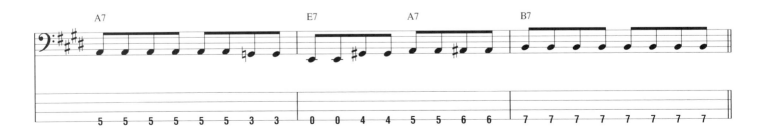

EXAMPLE 2

Let's pick up the tempo and do a bright, bumping shuffle so you can hear how effective this kind of feel can be. Notice the walk-down to the I chord in measure 6.

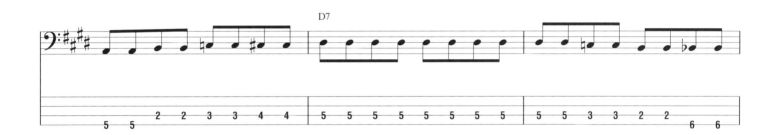

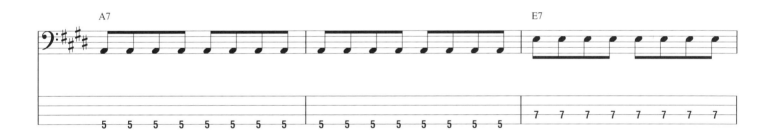

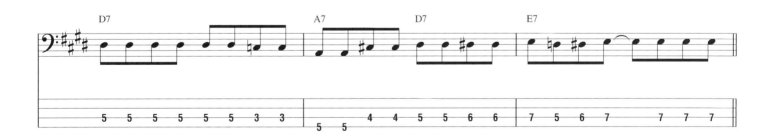

The root shuffle is a great way to support the band, plus it stays out of the way of a busy melody or an elaborate guitar part.

LESSON #9: SWING BLUES

Swing blues bass lines, or walking blues lines, are much like walking a bass part in jazz. Sometimes they are a little more repetitive, but the common formula is using quarter notes and walking through the changes. Swing lines create a melodic rise and fall and steady movement among the changes, lending support while also creating harmonic tension and complexity.

Walking

Walking bass lines follow the chord progression by using notes from the scale of each chord. The goal is to make your way from one chord to the next in a musical fashion, creating a smooth, walking sound. To create more sonically interesting parts, notes outside the scale can be used to transition into new chords or as passing tones to get to the next note in the scale. This usually (but not always) happens on beat 4, when transitioning into a new chord. If you are unfamiliar with all the scales and modes, I suggest reviewing them before you work on walking; it will really make this fun and exciting, rather than hard and overwhelming. A little knowledge can go a long way.

You'll notice that, when creating a walking part, the best way to outline the chord progression is by playing the root on beat 1, especially when going to the I, IV, or V chord or whenever a new chord appears. If you are on the I chord for several measures, you can use other chord tones on beat 1, such as the 3rd or the 5th. The goal is to imply the chord and keep the tonality in focus so the listener and other band members can hear the changes.

EXAMPLE 1

Here is a swing blues in the key of G. Notice the A♭ chromatic passing tone on beat 4 of measure 3, which transitions us to the note G (the root of G7) on the downbeat of measure 4. You will also notice chromatic passing notes in measures 4, 5, 8, 9, 11, and 12. These passing tones give the walking line fluidity and an interesting sound.

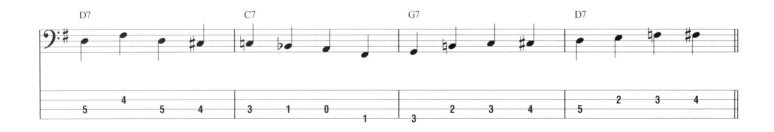

EXAMPLE 2

Here's another one in the key of G, but with a I–VI–II–V (G7–E7–A7–D7) progression. Take your time, and after you play the lines as written, try walking through the progression with your own walking bass part. In measure 7, notice that the notes are played twice. This is a great way to maintain movement without changing notes on every beat.

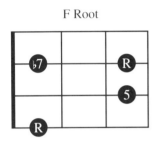

LESSON #10: THE BOX SHAPE

What's the box shape? It's a moveable four-note pattern on the fretboard that resembles a box; it consists of the root, 5th, ♭7th, and octave root.

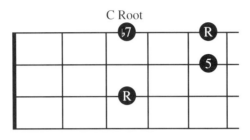
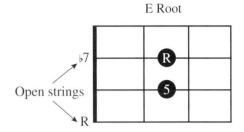

The great thing about the box shape is that the pattern stays the same for the I, IV, and V chord and it can be moved around the neck to play in any key!

Uptown

Sometimes referred to as the "uptown down" pattern, the uptown box pattern starts at the root and then ascends to the 5th, ♭7th, and octave root.

EXAMPLE 1

For this example, play each note short and tight.

EXAMPLE 2

Here is another way you can play the line.

Downtown

This next pattern is called the "downtown" box pattern, or "uptown up" line, because it starts on the root and then jumps up to the octave root before descending to the ♭7th and 5th.

EXAMPLE 3

EXAMPLES 4–5

Here are two triplet embellishments.

Other Box Patterns

Here are a few more typical box-shape shuffle patterns that you might come across. Although arranged here in the key of C, play through any 12-bar blues progression and adjust the patterns accordingly.

EXAMPLES 6–9

TWO-BEAT FEEL

The two-beat feel is great for country blues and any other simple but steady groove. The two-beat feel is comprised of the root on beat 1 and the 5th on beat 3 or the root on beats 1 and 3 and the 5th on beats 2 and 4, depending on the tempo. It's one of the oldest accompaniment patterns in music and can be heard in blues, jazz, folk, country, and most popular music.

EXAMPLE 1

Here is a basic two-beat example in the key of G.

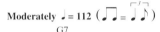

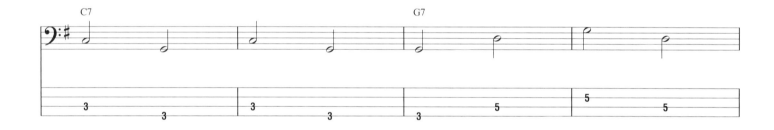
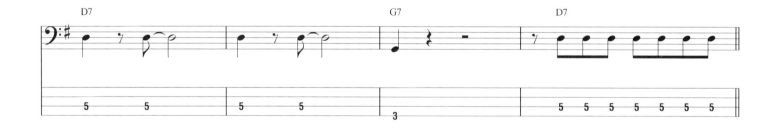

Common Fills

The great thing about bass is its role within the band; it brings together the harmony and the rhythm and can change the sound of a song. Fills are great for adding some anticipation, forecasting prior to the chord change, or for building movement when staying on one chord. A common fill for adding movement in the two-beat feel are chromatic walk-ups. For example, start a whole step away from the target note on beat 4 (when counting the root/5th pattern as quarter notes) and then walk up chromatically to the target note, whether it's the root of the I, IV, or V chord. If you are targeting the I chord, play the ♭7th on beat 4 and move chromatically to the major 7th on the upbeat, resolving to the root on beat 1. To walk up to the IV chord, use the ♭3rd on beat 4, moving chromatically to the major 3rd on the upbeat and resolving to the root of the IV chord on beat 1. And finally, to walk up to the V chord, play the 4th on beat 4, moving chromatically to the ♭5th (or ♯4th) on the upbeat and resolving to the root of the V chord on beat 1. If the song is played at a tempo at which you are counting the root/5th pattern as half notes, start the walk-up on beat 3 and play quarter notes.

EXAMPLE 2

Here is a great example of walk-up fills in the key of E.

Another common theme in a two beat, or two feel, is the use of the ♭7th on beat 4 of every other measure. Here is an example in the key of E. This is a sound that you will hear quite often and is a great way to change up the feel and add some character.

EXAMPLE 3

LESSON #12: PIVOT NOTE

To add some flow to a bass line or fill, incorporate a pivot, or anchor, note as a center point from which to bounce other notes off. The anchor is most often the root note or the 5th and is added in between the notes that you intend to play while you are walking up or down.

EXAMPLE 1

Below is an example of a standard walk-up that is played normally in the first two bars and then incorporates a root-note pivot point in measures 3–4 to add some bounce and keep the low G in the line.

EXAMPLE 2

Here is a standard ending that uses a pivot note. It should be quite familiar to your ears.

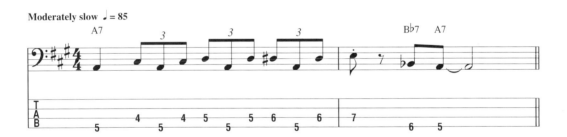

Barring

Playing each note with your finger tips or moving your fingers to another string isn't always convenient when using a pivot note. Sometimes you have to fret a note with another part of your finger, especially when it's available vertically under the currently fretted note. This is called barring. Barring requires you to straighten out your finger and play each note between the joints of the flattened finger.

EXAMPLE 3

Here is a technical exercise to help you execute some of the tricky fingerings without moving your hand. Play each fret with the same finger: first finger at fret 5, second finger at fret 6, and so on. Use your finger tips on the low string but flatten out your fingers and use the flattened part to fret the other notes.

EXAMPLE 4

For this next example, we'll play a blues-rock groove that uses a pivot for the main riff and for all the walk-ups. Go slow and take your time getting the barring clean.

LESSON #13: BOOGIE WOOGIE

Boogie woogie comes from the piano blues style of the early 20th century. Boogie bass lines outline the chord and are repetitive. The patterns are most often two bars long and always involve the root, 3rd, and 5th. Since the main pattern is two bars, a slight abbreviation occurs in measures 9 and 10 for the V and IV chord, respectively. This usually consists of cutting the line in half, following the same rule that is applied to songs that contain a quick change in measure 2.

EXAMPLE 1

Played here in the key of G, this boogie bass line, 1–3–5–6–♭7–6–5–3, is one of the most common lines in this style.

EXAMPLE 2

Here are the last six measures of the same boogie line. This time, however, eighth notes are used and the line is arranged in the key of E.

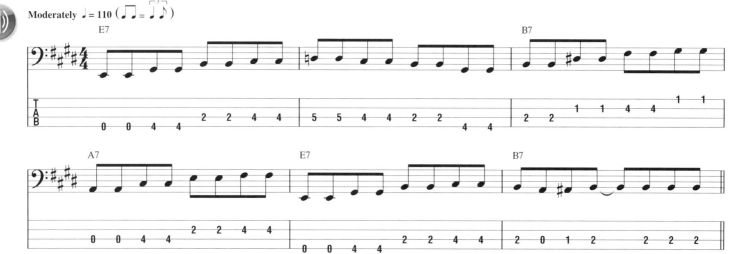

EXAMPLE 3

Another common line is: 1–3–5–6–8 (1)–6–5–3. Let's give it a try in the key of F!

Jump Blues

Jump blues is an uptempo style of swing that incorporates walking boogie bass lines. In this style, it's common to find a ii–V turnaround in measures 9–10 (instead of V–IV) and a I–VI–ii–V progression in measures 11–12. When people call a jump blues song, pick a quarter-note boogie line and kick it into gear!

EXAMPLE 4

This one's in the key of A♭.

LESSON #14: THE RHUMBA

In the blues, the rhumba is not the same as the Latin rumba. In the former, the rhumba describes a certain syncopated feel that came out of the musical melting pot known as New Orleans. The most basic feel starts on beat 1, followed by hits on the "and" of beat 2 and on beat 4. Let's get started.

EXAMPLE 1

Here is a rhumba in the key of G.

EXAMPLE 2

Here is another rhumba line that you hear most often in the blues. The bass line is heard in Albert King's "Crosscut Saw" and in renditions by B.B. King and Gary Moore of Tampa Red's song "Don't You Lie to Me." This one's in the key of B.

EXAMPLE 3

Let's do one more rhumba. This one's in the key of A. The tempo is faster and the pattern is played in different ways.

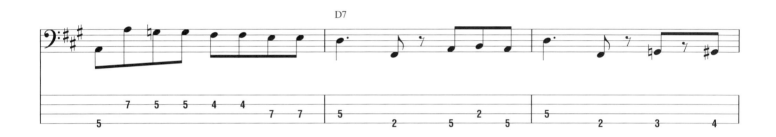

MINOR BLUES FORM

The minor blues form is a 12-bar blues written in a minor key. To get you started, we'll look at the most typical set of chord changes in the minor blues form. The best way to familiarize yourself with minor blues is to listen to recordings and learn as much as you can by analyzing and playing along.

12-Bar Minor Blues

The minor blues progression is much like a major 12-bar blues, but the I and IV chords are minor.

EXAMPLE 1

In this example, Roman numerals are written along with the chords in the key of C (lowercase numerals represent minor chords). Listen along so you can hear the changes.

EXAMPLE 2

This example is as common as the previous one, but uses all minor chords.

If you are familiar with "The Thrill Is Gone" by B.B. King, you might recognize the sound of these changes. My best advice is to learn several minor blues changes. Then, when one gets called on the bandstand, listen closely and it will all become clear.

EXAMPLE 3

Moderately slow ♩ = 80

Things to Keep in Mind

Here are some things to keep in mind so you aren't thrown off when someone calls for a minor blues on the bandstand. First, be on alert for the V chord in measure 12. Second, on occasion, just like in a standard 12-bar blues progression, the "quick four" (minor iv) shows up in measure 2 before going back to the i chord for measures 3–4. And lastly, stay away from the major 3rd when playing beneath minor chords!

LESSON #16: MINOR BLUES BASS LINES

In this lesson, we're going to explore some common bass lines for minor blues changes. If you are playing a walking bass line, all you need to do is walk within the changes. If you need to come up with a theme or bass part, below are some common examples to explore.

EXAMPLE 1

This one will sound familiar. It's a groove in the style of "Green Onions" by Booker T. & the MG's and a perfect example of a minor blues bass line—in this case, G minor.

EXAMPLE 2

Here is a line that works really well in slow- or medium-tempo minor blues songs. It's in the key of A minor.

EXAMPLE 3

This minor blues is in the key of F minor and played with a rhumba feel.

Performance Notes

When playing minor blues changes, if ever in doubt, play simple and don't be afraid to ask questions about the chord changes, bass lines, or form. It's OK not to know, and asking questions and being curious will enable you to do a good job, and that is what's important. Learning by experience, getting up there and trying, is a highly effective and meaningful approach to take in your quest to master the instrument. Having the desire to continuously seek out new information about your craft and asking questions will make you and your music better!

LESSON #17: FUNKY BLUES BASS LINES

Funk is a style with so many great bass lines that it's hard to pack them into a simple lesson. Like most blues bass lines, funk-blues lines are based on patterns or riffs and are usually played with a straight feel. Rest assured, as long as it's funky, the members of the band will be happy. With that being said, in most cases, keep your lines tight and stick to the pattern, because it's the main theme for the listener to dance to. If the audience is moving in their seats and on the dance floor, you are doing your job.

For this lesson, we'll start with a classic funk line that is similar to the groove in "Shotgun" by Junior Walker & the All Stars.

EXAMPLE 1

EXAMPLE 2

Here is another funky bass line; it's much like the Wilson Pickett cover of "Mustang Sally." You need to become familiar with this groove, especially if you play a blues gig!

Here are a few more examples of funky bass riffs. All of the examples are two-bar patterns (with repeats) for you to incorporate into a 12-bar form.

EXAMPLE 3

This one's in the key of A and uses some space over beat 4 of measure 1, which really helps the line breathe.

EXAMPLE 4

Here is the same riff played an octave higher.

EXAMPLE 5

This groove is in the key of E and starts with staccato notes on the downbeats.

Funky bass parts are sometimes improvised on the spot using the basic box pattern. Here are two funky bass lines that use the box shape in the key of G.

EXAMPLE 6

EXAMPLE 7

LESSON #18: BLUES-ROCK BASS LINES

It's easy to hear the major blues influence in rock music. Blues is at the root of almost all forms of popular music in the West. Blues-rock bass lines share several key elements with standard blues, but they are sometimes played without the shuffle or swing feel.

Rock 'n' roll originated in the late '40s and early '50s, evolving directly from blues. Another noticeable change prior to rock 'n' roll was the evolution of technology, particularly the electric guitar and amplifier, which are staples of rock music. In regard to bass, you'll notice some of the same bass lines played in both blues and rock, with a slightly faster tempo in the latter.

EXAMPLE 1

This example is in the key of E and is much like the groove in "Rocket 88" by Jackie Brenston.

EXAMPLE 2

Here is another familiar rock 'n' roll groove in E.

Blues rock is a 12-bar form over a rock feel, complete with improvisation and highly focused on the electric guitar. The style came about in the mid-'60s in England and the United States.

EXAMPLE 3

This one's in the key of A and is a box-shape pattern. Notice how it feels when it's played straight, versus a shuffle feel.

Below are a few more examples of blues-rock bass lines. All of them are two-bar examples (with repeats) for you to incorporate into a 12-bar form.

EXAMPLE 4

EXAMPLE 5

EXAMPLE 6

LESSON #19:
12/8 SLOW BLUES: THE QUICK FOUR

Slow blues is an important feel in the blues genre. Counted as 12 swinging eighth notes, it is a favorite feel for most blues ballads. If you play a blues gig, you can bet a 12/8 slow blues will be called, so it's best to have a few different bass lines in your repertoire. Due to the tempo of the slow blues, being solid and consistent with good note choices is of great importance because any mistakes are transparent. The "quick four" is a common chord change in a 12/8 slow blues.

Meat and Potatoes

When playing a 12/8 blues, there are many nuances—walk-ups, walk-downs, fills, and other subtleties—in addition to the "meat and potatoes" bass line. To give you some basic patterns to build from, the following examples represent the first four bars of a 12-bar blues in the key of C.

EXAMPLE 1

EXAMPLE 2

EXAMPLE 3

Here is the previous line with one small change: on beat 4 (or beat 10) we go to the 3rd, instead of the 6th.

EXAMPLE 4

EXAMPLE 5

This example is a variation on the previous bass line, omitting the walk-down on beat 4 (beat 10) in favor of staying on the 6th.

EXAMPLE 6

EXAMPLE 7

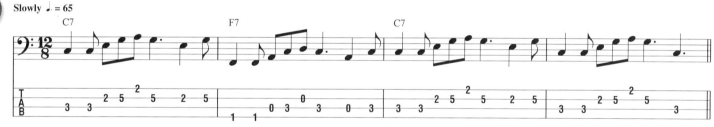

12/8 SLOW BLUES: THE 12-BAR FORM

Here are some full, 12-bar slow blues examples with the quick four to practice. Pay attention to the chord changes and check out the use of chord tones and chromatic walk-ups and walk-downs transitioning to the I, IV, and V chords.

EXAMPLE 1

EXAMPLE 2

Listen and Watch

Since blues is a highly improvisational form of music, it requires big ears and big eyes. Listen and watch for dynamic cues from the soloist and other band members. These cues can show up via verbal language or body language, so one must listen and watch. The dynamic between band and soloist is much like cooking a meal together. Imagine the soloist is the head chef and it's the band's job to add the ingredients and create the chef's vision. The band is familiar with the basic meal but, on the bandstand, things ebb and flow, so the band must follow and adapt by matching intensity. To create the chef's vision, the band must be conscious of the flame's intensity and whether they should back off and let things cool down. The band must know when to add ingredients or when to leave things alone. Improvisation is a mutual creation, and that is what makes the blues so much fun to play.

LESSON #21: "STORMY MONDAY" CHANGES

The T-Bone Walker song "Call It Stormy Monday (But Tuesdays Is Just as Bad)," which is usually referred to as simply "Stormy Monday," is a commonly played blues standard and a great song to know, especially if you plan on playing the blues. Over the years, the chord changes for this song have evolved from the original. In 1961, Bobby Bland recorded his interpretation of the song, adding some chord substitutions that became a template for the Allman Brothers' version, which is perhaps the most popular version of the song today.

EXAMPLE 1

This example contains the most commonly used changes to "Stormy Monday." If you're familiar with these changes and listen closely to the band, you'll be fine. If you are unsure about the progression, be sure to ask about measures 9–10, where a ii–iv change is substituted for a standard V–IV progression.

The Last Four Bars

When playing the chord changes to "Stormy Monday," be aware that variations frequently occur in measures 9 and 10—people play these bars differently—which is why you'll need to pay close attention to the band.

EXAMPLE 2

This example represents the last six measures of "Stormy Monday." Notice that, in measure 10, the progression moves to a ♭VI7–V7 (E♭7–D7) change, with each chord lasting two beats.

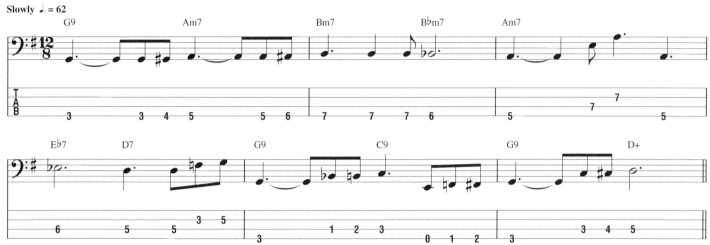

EXAMPLE 3

Another common change in measure 9 is to go to the V7 chord, instead of the ii chord. Here it is, starting from measure 7.

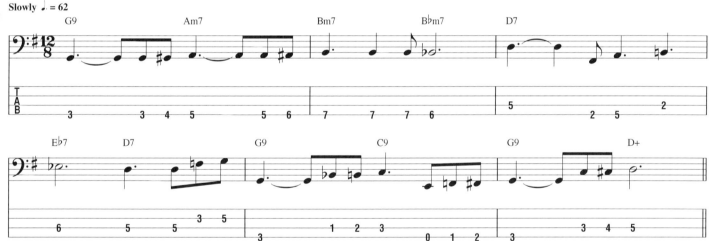

EXAMPLE 4

Typically, the last two bars consist of a I7–IV7–I7–V7 progression, with the final chord (V7) voiced as an augmented triad, as illustrated in the previous examples, rather than a dominant seventh chord.

LESSON #22: DEAD NOTES

Dead notes are muted notes without pitch; they are played as a percussive effect to "move air" or add a "thump" sound to any bass line. To execute a dead note, lightly touch the string with your fret hand (without pushing it down to the fretboard) and pluck. Be mindful not to touch the string directly over the fret wire, which might result in a harmonic. What we are looking for is a dead/percussive sound.

Exercises

To get familiar with playing dead notes, let's work on a few blues-flavored exercises, which are for practicing the technique, not substitutes for actual bass lines. Once you become well-versed in dead-note technique, it will start to show up in your playing.

EXAMPLE 1

This one incorporates dead notes on the same string as the fully fretted pitches. Work on it at the indicated tempo (86 bpm), gradually increasing your speed. Play the dead notes with the same dynamic as the fretted pitches.

EXAMPLE 2

For this next exercise, play the dead note on the lower, adjacent string to add a deeper-sounding "thump."

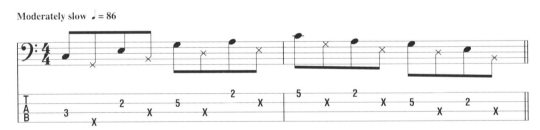

EXAMPLE 3

Now we'll attack the higher string for a brighter-sounding dead note.

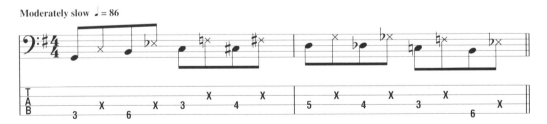

Come up with your own exercises by turning any quarter-note bass line into an eighth-note pattern by adding a dead note after each fretted pitch.

Dead-Note Grooves

Here are some blues examples that incorporate dead notes. While dead notes are really common in walking bass lines, adding too many can make a line too jumpy or choppy, so use them judiciously.

EXAMPLE 4

The next two examples are two-bar grooves that can be played over a 12-bar blues.

EXAMPLE 5

EXAMPLE 6

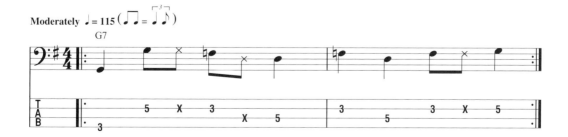

LESSON #23: GUITAR ARRANGEMENT FOR BASS

As a bassist, it's fun to explore non-traditional ways to play the instrument, like playing guitar chords on bass. Why, you might ask? Many early recordings used two guitars but no bass. Even Jimi Hendrix's 1966 recording of the song "Red House" was recorded with two guitars and no bass. In this lesson, we'll explore some guitar parts that can be adapted to bass.

EXAMPLE 1

For this example, we are playing a shuffle that incorporates the root, 5th, 6th, and ♭7th of each chord. This one is a slow blues in the key of A and can be used for songs like "Red House."

EXAMPLE 2

Now let's play a similar bass part in the key of E and speed it up to a moderate shuffle.

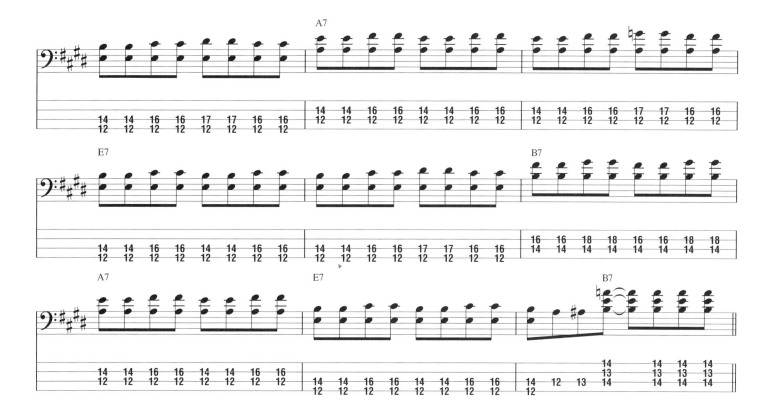

EXAMPLE 3

This next example is a simple accompaniment (also called "comping") exercise for playing in a duo format. You can use it for the solo section in place of a walking bass line or pattern. It consists of playing the root on beats 1 and 3 and the chords on beats 2 and 4.

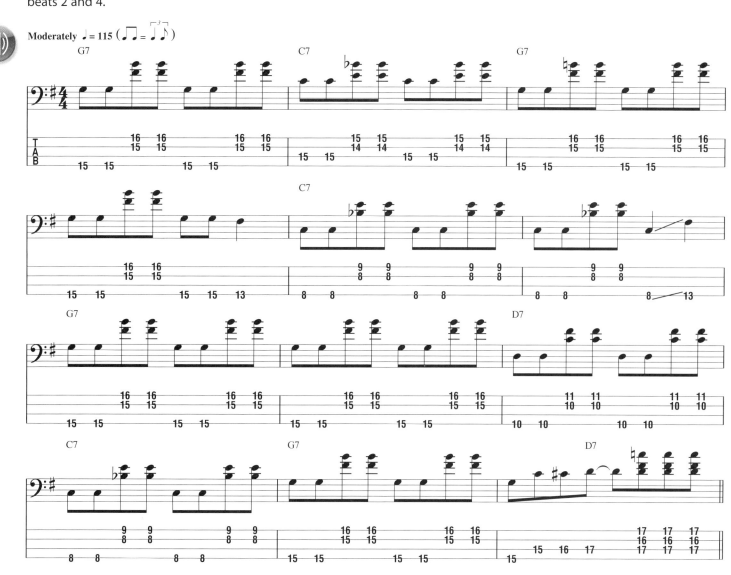

LESSON #24: SLIDES

Slides are a great way to loosen things up and add some character, vibe, and grease to a line. Slide technique is executed by striking a note and sliding your finger up or down the string without releasing pressure. Slides, like many other coloration techniques, are a way to change up the standard way of getting around the fretboard. Sliding into a note has a far different sound than just picking it, and when used tastefully, can add a cool sound.

Sliding Around

There are two types of slides. One is an in-time slide, which is just a regular slide with rhythmic value; the other is a grace-note slide, which contains no rhythmic value and is notated with—you got it—a grace note.

EXAMPLE 1

For the first example, we'll incorporate both types of slides.

Blues Bass Lines

Let's take a look at some bass lines that sound much different when played with a slide. Both ways work great; it's really just a matter of personal preference.

EXAMPLE 2

Here's a blues rhumba in the key of B♭ played with (measure 3–4) and without (measure 1–2) a slide.

EXAMPLE 3

Here is a standard boogie line in the key of G. After four measures of steady quarter notes, slides are incorporated into the second half of the line.

EXAMPLE 4

This bass line is similar to the rhumba example, but the slide is played in time to give it a slightly different feel.

EXAMPLE 5

Slides are great when walking up a line. Here is a funky Chicago-style blues with a walk-up.

Listen to great blues players of all kinds, not just bass, and notice how they attack, slide, bend, hammer on, pull off, and use vibrato, all of which are technical colorations to add to the feel and expression of your instrument.

LESSON #25: HAMMER-ONS

Hammer-ons are a legato technique that give you another way to play two or more notes. Instead of plucking each note, the hammer-on enables you to pluck the first and hammer on to the second, creating a more fluid sound. To play a hammer-on, place one of your fingers on a fret and pluck that note. While the note is ringing, "hammer" another finger onto a higher fret on the same string, sounding the note without plucking it. When you get used to this technique, you can string together more than two notes and create that smooth, flowing sound. It also enables you to play really fast without having to pluck each note.

Put the Hammer Down

EXAMPLE 1

Let's play an exercise to get started. Play a G note at the fifth fret of the D string with your first finger and then hammer on to the seventh-fret A note with your third finger. To get an even sound, work at maintaining the volume between the plucked and hammered notes.

EXAMPLE 2

Now we'll try three notes.

EXAMPLE 3

Let's move on to four notes.

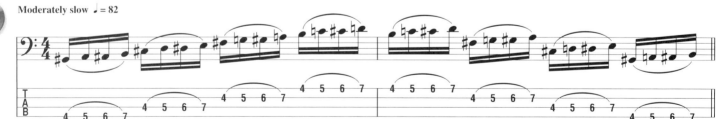

Blues Bass Lines

EXAMPLE 4

Here are the first six bars of a rhumba in the key of A. A hammer-on is used on beat 4 of each measure.

EXAMPLE 5

This one's a blues-rock example in the key of A. It might sound familiar, as it's much like the Doors' "Roadhouse Blues."

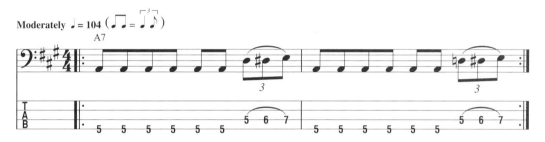

EXAMPLE 6

Here are the first six bars of blues in C. The bass line has a distinct two-beat feel.

Sometimes songs will have a unison line that you can embellish slightly or, if you are playing a fill, try starting with a hammer-on to give it a different vibe. Below is a four-note pattern that is played normally and then played with a hammer-on on beat 1.

EXAMPLE 7

LESSON #26: PULL-OFFS

Pull-offs can be thought of as the opposite of hammer-ons, but the technique is actually considerably different. To play a pull-off, fret two notes simultaneously on the same string, pluck the higher note, and then pull off with that finger in a downward motion, thereby causing the pre-fretted lower note to sound. This can be a little tricky and will take some finger and hand strength to execute, so take your time and work it out until it's comfortable to play and sounds nice and clean. Practice makes patterns, so it's best to practice things slowly in order to develop good patterns.

Pull It Off

EXAMPLE 1

It's best to start with an exercise. Place your third finger on the D note at the seventh fret of the G string and, and at the same time, place your first finger on the C note at the fifth fret. Pluck the D note and then pull off the third finger in a downward motion to sound the C.

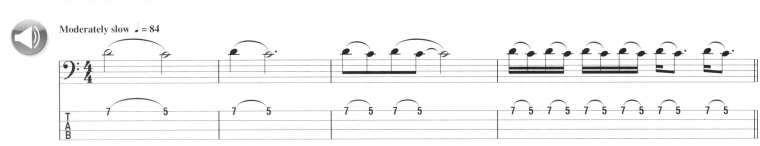

EXAMPLE 2

This next exercise is a little tricky. Take your time and place all three fingers on the string before pulling off.

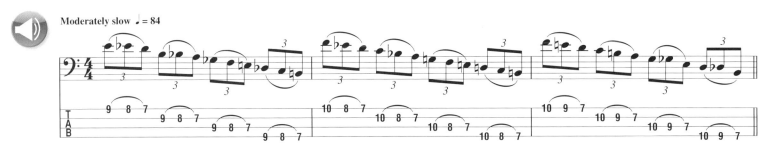

Building up finger strength to perform four-finger pull-offs takes some time, especially the pinky. Therefore, take some time to practice two-finger pull-offs, starting with your pinky and index finger before moving on to your pinky and middle and pinky and ring finger.

EXAMPLE 3

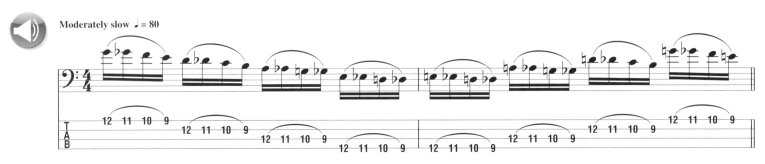

Blues Bass Lines

EXAMPLE 4

Practicing bass lines is a great way to work on grooving and new techniques. Here are the first six bars of a funky 12-bar groove in the key of C that incorporates both pull-offs and hammer-ons.

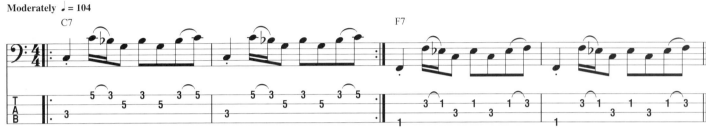

EXAMPLE 5

This one's a 12/8 blues in the key of C. We'll do the first six bars of this 12-bar blues as well.

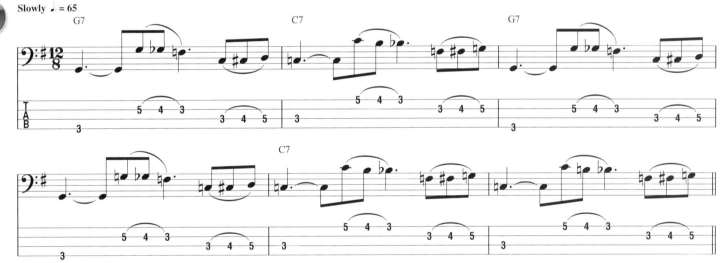

EXAMPLE 6

This next example is a lick that can be used to solo over the key of A. It incorporates a combination of hammer-ons and pull-offs, which are great for soloing and playing fills.

LESSON #27: GRACE NOTES

Grace notes are musical ornaments, or embellishments, that usually are not part of the piece of music that you are playing. Grace notes hold no rhythmic value. What they do is add a stylistic component to the music to give character and personalize what would normally be played the same by everyone. While grace notes may be added by the composer to achieve a specific sound, they are usually added by the performer. In blues bass, grace notes can be a great way to personalize a part and add a bend-like approach to any note that you are playing.

Execution

Grace notes can be played with various techniques, including hammer-ons, pull-offs, slides, and bends. Let's take a look at all of these techniques within the same line.

EXAMPLE 1

Slowly ♩ = 74

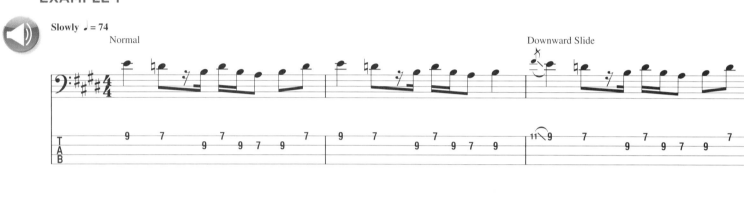

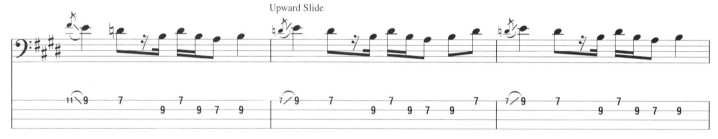

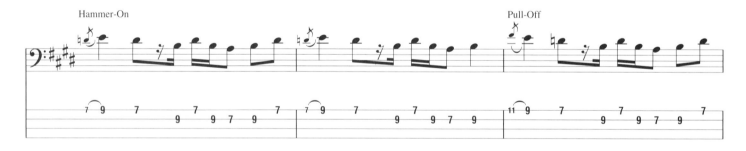

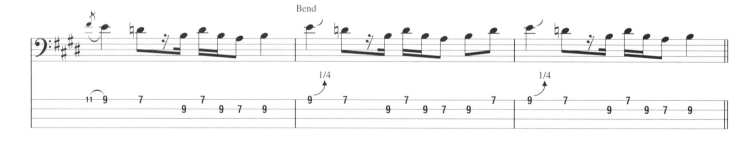

Bass Lines

The bass lines below are played normally for two bars and then embellished with a grace note.

EXAMPLE 2

This one's a funky blues in the key of A.

EXAMPLE 3

In measures 3–4 of this rhumba, a ♭3rd grace note is hammered on to the major 3rd to give the line a real bluesy feel.

EXAMPLE 4

This shuffled bass line features a quick, grace-note hammer-on from the 6th to the ♭7th.

EXAMPLE 5

This 12/8 slow blues gets some additional grease in measures 3–4 via grace-note slides.

LESSON #28: THE MIXOLYDIAN MODE

The Mixolydian mode, sometimes referred to as the "dominant scale," is built from the fifth degree of the major scale. It contains all the same notes as the major scale, except for the 7th, which is lowered by a semitone (one half step). The formula for the Mixolydian mode is: 1–2–3–4–5–6–♭7. It is a great scale to use over dominant chords because it contains all four chord tones (1–3–5–♭7).

EXAMPLE 1

Here is the C Mixolydian mode in its moveable shape.

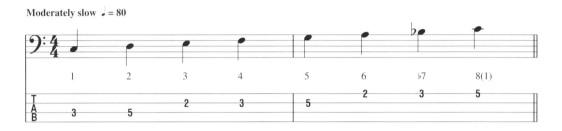

Here is another way to look at the moveable shape for the Mixolydian mode.

EXAMPLE 2

Let's play the A Mixolydian mode in two octaves.

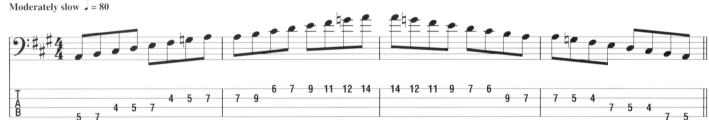

Chords

The symbol for a dominant chord is represented by a letter and the number 7 (e.g., C7, D7, A7, and E7). Dominant chords are built from the root, 3rd, 5th, and ♭7th of their relative Mixolydian mode.

Bass Lines

If this is your first lesson on the Mixolydian mode, it may come as a surprise that you probably have played bass parts that are based on the Mixolydian mode. For example, box-shape bass patterns are built from the root, 5th, ♭7th, and octave root of the scale.

Here are some examples. The first three are moderate shuffles.

EXAMPLE 3

EXAMPLE 4

EXAMPLE 5

EXAMPLE 6

This one's a boogie line.

A Note on Soloing

If you are a soloing bassist, the Mixolydian mode may sound a little jazzy, especially for some traditional blues players, but it sounds really great when mixed with the blues scale and other pentatonic scales. Give it a try!

GROOVE TIP: ACCENT ON BEATS 2 AND 4

When playing the blues, one thing is for sure: if it's grooving, everyone is moving. Groove, or feel, comes quite naturally for some; for others, it's something they have to work on. Even if something comes naturally, exploring all aspects of music and how one might evolve and improve is beneficial. The great thing about music is that it's a constantly evolving relationship that never ends.

Accent

For this lesson, we'll look at the dynamic accent (>), which indicates that the marked note should be played louder. Accents are often overlooked because they're such a subtle thing, but becoming aware of how you place accents in a bass part can make a huge difference in your groove. Let's start with an exercise. We can talk all day, but when it comes to music, playing is the best language one can speak.

EXAMPLE 1

For most blues shuffles, it's best to accent on beats 2 and 4. This accents the snare and will help far more than you might imagine, especially if you aren't playing with a drummer. Let's explore this idea by showing contrast. The first four bars of this first example are played without accents. Then, in measures 5–8, accents are added to beats 2 and 4.

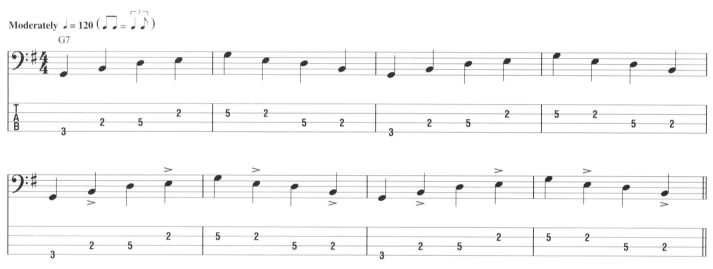

EXAMPLE 2

Let's play a box-shape blues shuffle pattern and concentrate on laying the accents on beats 2 and 4.

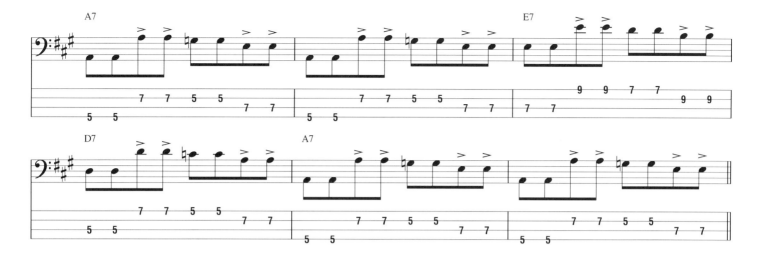

EXAMPLE 3

Here's a minor blues.

EXAMPLE 4

Accents work especially well on walking bass parts.

LESSON #30: PALM MUTING

Palm muting is a technique that is used for changing the timbre of the bass and for muting the strings. Are you looking for a more traditional sound that is short, thumpy, and tubby? Then palm muting is what you are looking for. It can be used for a quieter part when the dynamics of a song change, or if you like the sound, the whole song.

Execution

To palm mute, rest the palm of your plucking hand on the strings, towards the bridge, making sure the hand rests just over the strings. To pluck the strings, you can use your thumb, a pick, or if you prefer, a combination of your thumb and fingers. The closer to the bridge you are, the more the strings will ring. If you want a more muted tone, move your palm closer to the neck. Experiment with the location until you find what sounds the best to you.

Bass Lines

Let's start with some contrast by playing several bass lines that are performed with and without palm muting. That way, you can hear the difference. Palm muting is noted with a "P.M." between the notation and tab staves.

EXAMPLE 1

If you want to sound traditional, try palm muting a 1–3–5–6 line.

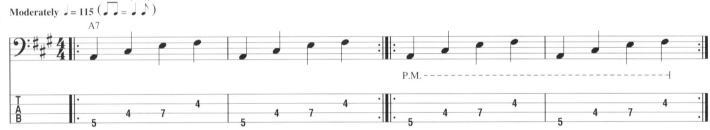

EXAMPLE 2

Here's a rhumba in the key of D. I love playing rhumbas with a palm mute.

EXAMPLE 3

This one's a blues-rock line.

EXAMPLE 4

A "bump" in F sounds great using a slight palm mute.

EXAMPLE 5

Palm mutes sound great on a slow blues. As the song builds during a solo, lessen the palm muting.

Vibrato and bending are not techniques that make you think about the bass, but they are a huge part of blues guitar. Nonetheless, vibrato is an essential technique for almost all stringed instruments, and bass is no exception. Bending on bass is less common but can be used for soloing or an occasional fill.

Vibrato

Vibrato is a great technique for adding expression to your playing and it can range from really subtle to overt. A slight vibrato on long notes in a slow blues is great on occasion, and vibrato in a nice, melodic blues solo can really add a vocal quality to the sound. Let's look at the three types of bass vibrato.

Bend Vibrato: This is achieved by pushing the string up (toward the ceiling) and pulling it down (toward the floor), using your wrist in a rotating motion, back and forth, or using your forearm. With this type of vibrato, the pitch will fluctuate between slightly sharp and in tune.

Pivot Vibrato: This vibrato works well on fretless bass but isn't very noticeable on fretted bass. It is achieved by pivoting your fretting finger toward the nut and then toward the bridge in a rolling-type fashion. The pitch will fluctuate between slightly sharp, in tune, and slightly flat.

Shake: A shake is like a pivot vibrato and a slide combined. Instead of rolling your finger, you rapidly slide your finger over the fret wire, back and forth, creating a very noticeable slurring sound.

EXAMPLE 1

In this first example, all three vibratos are played twice; first time, subtly, and then more pronounced. Pivot vibrato is performed on fretless bass.

EXAMPLE 2

Here are the first six bars of a slow blues in G. A little vibrato is used on beats 1 and 3. Be sure to keep the vibrato subtle so the pitch doesn't stay consistently sharp.

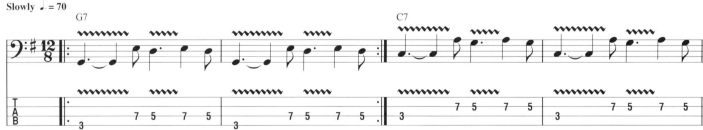

EXAMPLE 3

Here's a lick that you can use when soloing. The first two bars use regular vibrato, followed in measures 3–4 by a shake on beat 3.

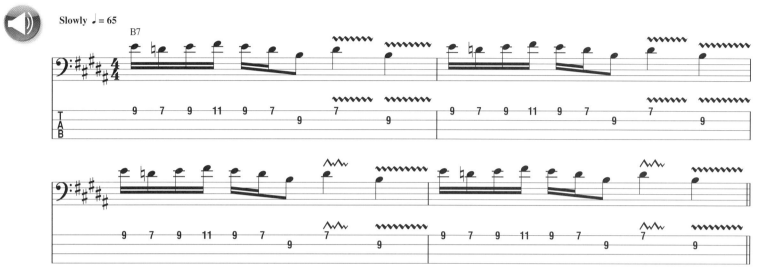

EXAMPLE 4

Let's explore another lead lick that incorporates vibrato.

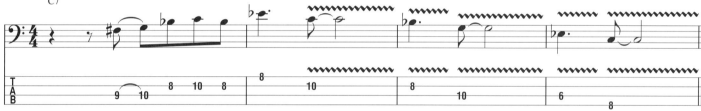

EXAMPLE 5

Let's try vibrato up high on the neck.

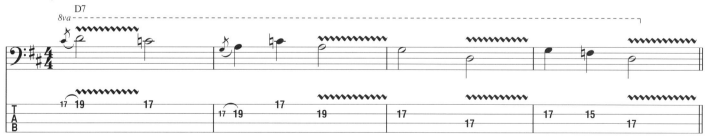

LESSON #32: PASSING TONES

Passing tones, or chromatic passing notes, are notes that are not in the key of the song being played or are notes outside the scale that fit with the chord being played. Passing tones are used to walk up or down to the target note. You can also think of passing tones as notes that can be added in between the notes in a scale. For example, let's say the bass plays G on beat 4 and the target note is an F (beat 1). To create a sense of movement, harmonically and rhythmically, a G♭ would be the perfect note because it's the closest to F (from G) and gives the listener a sense of what's to come. Basically, passing tones forecast to the ear what is to come. Passing tones are used all the time in jazz and blues bass lines, among other musical styles.

EXAMPLE 1

Here is a 12-bar blues in the key of B♭. Notice that all of the chords are dominant. That means that the scale we will be using is the Mixolydian mode. All of the passing tones are circled so you can easily identify them and see how they are used to transition into target notes.

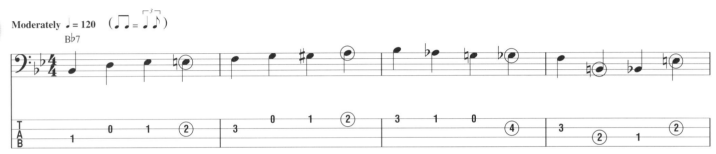
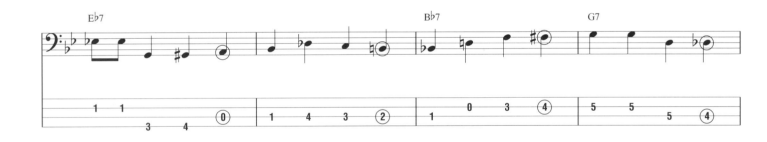
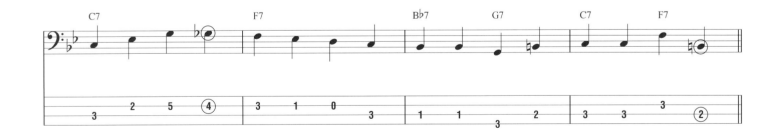

Strong and Weak Beats

For walking bass lines in 4/4 time, consider beats 1 and 3 the strong beats and beats 2 and 4 the weak beats. The strong beats, or stressed beats, are the places where you want to play notes that define the harmony you are playing. For example, playing the root on beat 1 is a great start, as are the 3rd or 5th. For beat 3, any chord tone will work. What this does is solidify the harmony to the other musicians and listener. For the weak beats, or unstressed beats, you can play pretty much any note since the harmony is stated by chord tones on the strong beats. When outlining a chord, playing notes from the scale on weak beats adds congruency, but chromatic notes work fine as well. When walking a line, just keep in mind that your job as a bassist is to outline the chord changes and create lines that are flowing and smooth.

EXAMPLE 2

This next example is for you to compose a walking bass part over a 12-bar blues in G. Keep in mind the concept of strong and weak beats and write the notes in the music staves provided.

Moderately ♩ = 120

G7

C7   G7   E7

A7   D7   G7

LESSON #33: THE MAJOR PENTATONIC SCALE

Penta is a Greek prefix meaning "five," and a pentatonic scale is a five-note scale (per octave), which is two fewer than standard seven-note major and minor scales. The major pentatonic scale is constructed from the first, second, third, fifth, and sixth degrees of the major scale (1–2–3–5–6). Although it may seem like an incomplete major scale, it does have its own tonality.

Circle of 5ths

Another way to think of the major pentatonic scale is to build it from the circle of 5ths. All you have to do is pick a note, which will serve as the root, and then move through the circle of 5ths clockwise for five notes. The result is a major pentatonic scale. For the C major pentatonic scale, start on C and then move (in 5ths) through the next four notes: C, G, D, A, and E. Rearranged, these notes spell out the C major pentatonic scale: C–D–E–G–A. Start on A and you get the A major pentatonic scale: A–E–B– F♯–C♯ (in order: A–B–C♯–E–F♯). This is why the major pentatonic scale sounds so strong and is a great choice for blues bass lines and soloing.

EXAMPLE 1

Here is the C major pentatonic scale. To change keys, simply move the pattern up or down the neck.

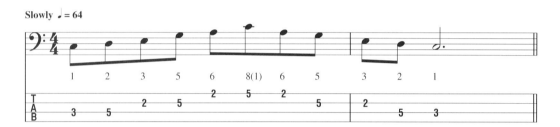

Here is another way to look at the moveable shape for the major pentatonic scale.

Bass Lines

Let's look at some bass lines that revolve around the major pentatonic scale.

EXAMPLE 2

Here is a shuffle that outlines the A major pentatonic scale, minus the 2nd.

EXAMPLE 3

Here is a line in the style of the song "My Girl" by the Temptations, demonstrating the major pentatonic scale in an R&B-style blues.

EXAMPLE 4

Here's a boogie line that outlines the F major pentatonic scale, minus the 2nd.

Soloing

When soloing over a blues, the major pentatonic scale is a great start for melodic material. It's not as bluesy as you might want, but it creates a nice, open, solid sound.

For this 12-bar blues in A, use the A major pentatonic scale over the I chord and the D major pentatonic scale over the IV chord. Notice that the A and D major pentatonic scales share four notes: A, B, E, and F♯. For the V chord, use the E major pentatonic scale.

Make up melodies over the changes with each scale and change the rhythms and order of the notes—much like walking a bass part, but more broken up and melodic. This is a great way to practice soloing.

EXAMPLE 5

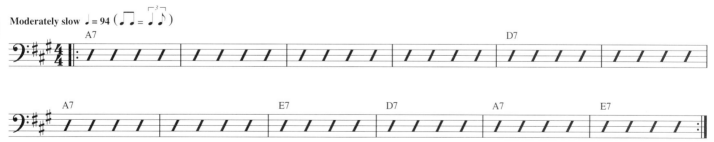

LESSON #34: THE MINOR PENTATONIC SCALE

The minor pentatonic scale is built from the first, third, fourth, fifth, and seventh degrees of the natural minor scale (1–3–4–5–7). If you looked at it from the perspective of the major scale, the minor pentatonic scale is spelled: 1–♭3–4–5–♭7. The great thing about using a minor pentatonic scale over the blues is that it gives you the root, 5th, and ♭7th of a dominant chord, plus the ♭3rd, which is a "blue" note.

EXAMPLE 1

Here is the C minor pentatonic scale. To change keys, simply move the pattern up or down the neck.

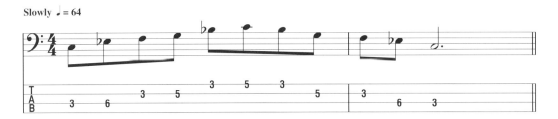

Here's another way to look at the moveable shape for the minor pentatonic scale.

Relationships

The minor pentatonic and major pentatonic scales have a relative relationship. The fifth note of the major pentatonic scale is a major 6th above the root, and that fifth note is the root note of the relative minor pentatonic scale. You could also look at the second note of the minor pentatonic as the root of the relative major pentatonic scale.

EXAMPLE 2

Let's look at the E minor pentatonic scale and its relationship to the G major pentatonic scale. As you can see, they have the same pitches, just different starting notes.

Bass Lines

EXAMPLE 3

Here is a 12-bar minor blues that uses a minor pentatonic bass line.

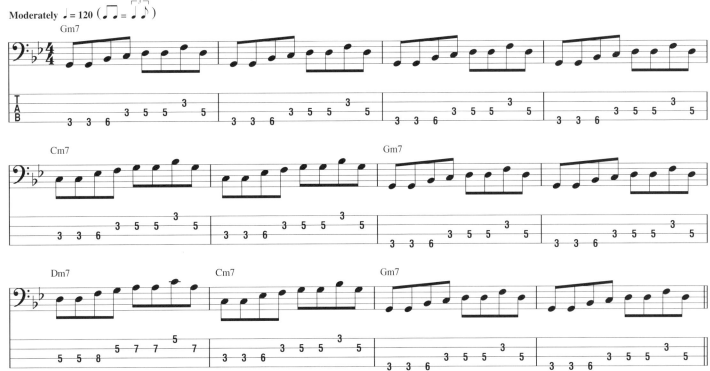

Soloing

For soloing over a blues, the minor pentatonic scale is great all around. It has a nice bluesy feel because of the ♭3rd and ♭7th. For this 12-bar blues in G, use the G minor pentatonic scale over the I chord, the C minor pentatonic scale over the IV chord, and the D minor pentatonic scale over the V chord. Another option is to stay on G minor pentatonic throughout. There will be some dissonant notes, but if you have melodic sensibilities, you can find the notes that work.

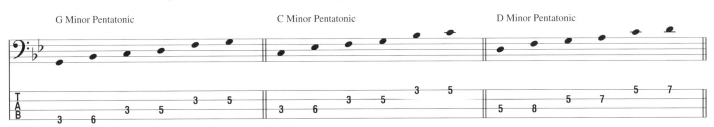

EXAMPLE 4

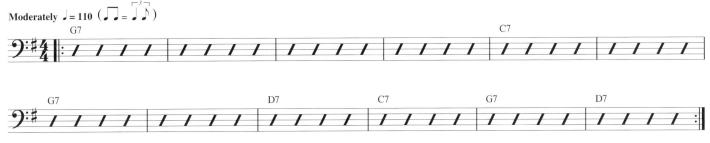

THE COMPOSITE BLUES SCALE

The composite blues scale is a nine-note scale: 1–2–♭3–3–4–♭5–5–6–♭7. Depending on your perspective, the composite blues scale is either a combination of the major pentatonic and the blues scales or a combination of the blues scale and the Mixolydian mode.

SCALE DEGREE:	1	2	♭3	3	4	♭5	5	6	♭7
C Composite Blues	C	D	E♭	E	F	G♭	G	A	B♭
C Blues	C		E♭		F	G♭	G		B♭
C Major Pentatonic	C	D		E			G	A	
C Mixolydian	C	D		E	F		G	A	B♭

EXAMPLE 1

Here's the C composite blues scale.

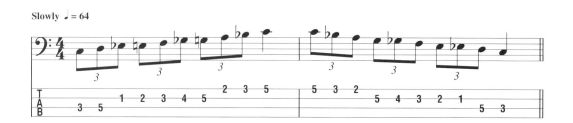

Application

The composite blues scale is great for playing and soloing over dominant seventh, ninth, or 13th chords, as well as altered dominant chords due to the presence of the ♭3rd, 3rd, ♭5th, and ♭7th.

Bass Lines

Let's play a shuffle in C. Instead of a V–IV turnaround, a II–V is used. Listen for the classic ascending/descending line in bars 9–10, which walks up the composite blues scale over the II chord and walks down the Mixolydian mode over the V chord.

EXAMPLE 2

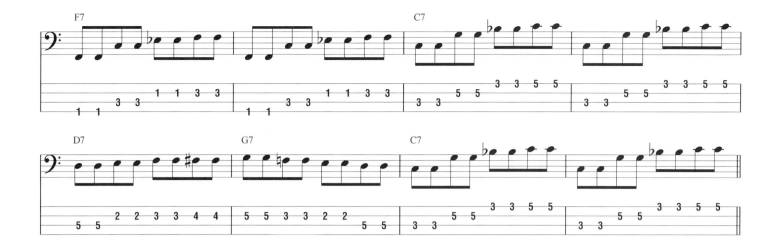

Soloing

Soloing over a blues with the composite blues scale gives you more note choices but it also can be a bit trickier to navigate. Since it contains notes that will clash when you land on them at the wrong time, it's best to spend time playing over chords and experimenting with ways to use the notes in lines that you develop. Playing scales is about building a musical vocabulary so that you can speak fluidly and know what you are saying. Feeling your way through chord changes is beneficial, but you want to be able to articulate a musical thought because it's something you know and have heard.

Here is a 12-bar blues in the key of C to practice the composite blues scale over. Try using the C composite blues scale over the entire progression before working out the F and G composite blues scales over the IV and V chords, respectively. Again, the goal is for you to practice making music by creating melodies with the information provided.

EXAMPLE 3

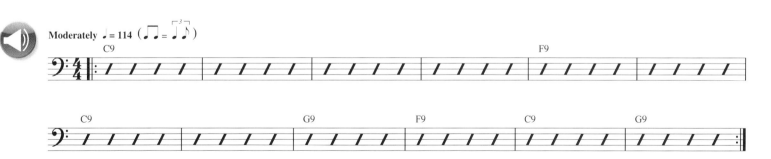

LESSON #36: STRING BENDING

String bending enables bassists to mimic the scooped notes of the human voice, as well as to hit pitches that fall in between the fretted notes. Bending the string raises the pitch. The farther you bend, the higher the pitch increase.

To bend, push the string up toward the ceiling or pull down toward the floor with the tip of your finger and hold it until the desired pitch is achieved. Bends can also be returned to their original pitch (i.e., released). Due to the larger strings on bass, quarter- and half-step bends are most common.

Let's work on a few bends. The next few examples are played twice; first, without a bend, and then with a bend.

EXAMPLE 1

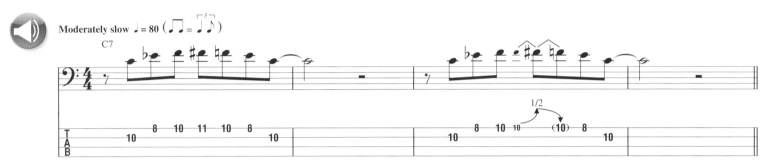

EXAMPLE 2

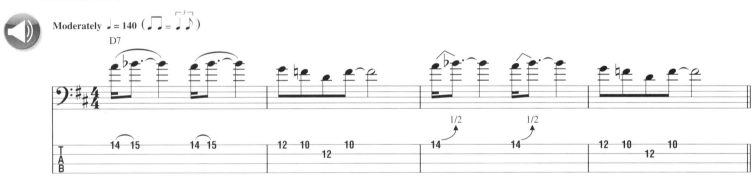

EXAMPLE 3

Now let's look at some quarter-step bends.

EXAMPLE 4

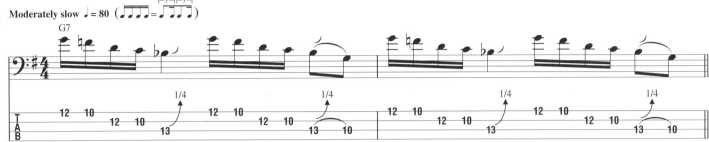

EXAMPLE 5

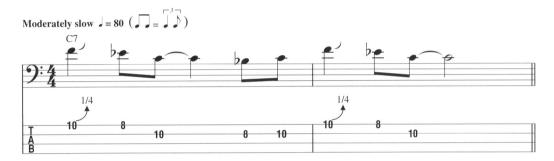

Emulating Vocalists

If you plan on soloing, one thing that really helps add feel, character, and a lyrical aspect to your playing is transcribing vocal melodies and playing them on bass. Most vocalists are noticeably different and have all kinds of little embellishments like bending notes and adding vibrato. Taking the time to learn and translate those subtleties on the bass can really help you learn new lines, patterns, and technical nuances. If you want to play great melodies in your solos, it only makes sense to play melodies on bass. The more you work on or play something, the more it becomes second nature.

LESSON #37: PRACTICING

Practicing is a necessary process of any skill. It's the process of doing something repeatedly with the goal of improving performance. You could also look at practicing like cultivating a relationship. Life is full of relationships—you have relationships with loved ones, family, friends, and the world around you. You even have a relationship with yourself (body, mind, etc.). Music is a relationship as well, and the time you spend working on and thinking about music is how you cultivate it. Your skills as a musician develop the more you consciously work at improving the relationship. How we spend our time is a reflection of what we think about, and it's how we spend our time that directly impacts the future. Practicing makes patterns, and patterns are the little actions that shape your life.

Types of Practice

When it comes to practicing, there are several areas of music to explore. You will notice that all players excel at different areas of music, and it all depends upon the individual. It's much like Howard Gardner's *Theory of Multiple Intelligences*.

Different Types of Intelligences

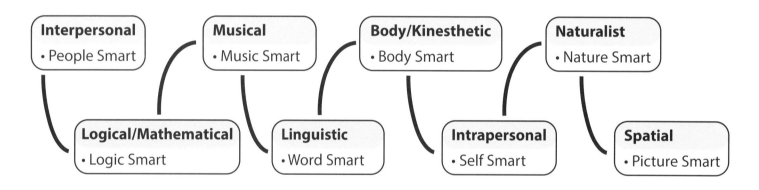

This model is about recognizing how all people are intelligent in different ways and intelligence is expressed in a variety of forms. According to Gardner, each individual possesses his or her own unique blend of all the intelligences, showing dominance and weakness in areas specific to the individual. For example, some people are more logical and understanding theory may come easier than to the person who tends to be more kinesthetic. The person who is more kinesthetic may have a great groove because they feel it in their body, while another might write great lyrics because they are linguistically intelligent and able to articulate how they feel (i.e., intrapersonal).

Practicing can be broken down into several areas to help you recognize what modalities or areas are your strong points and what areas are your weaknesses. Here are five examples:

Technical: The ability to move your fingers over the strings of an instrument. The more proficient you are at technique, the more freely you will be able to express your musical ideas without limitations.

Mental: The ability to understand or comprehend notes, scales, theory, and musical concepts. The more you understand, the easier it is to communicate musically.

Auditory: The ability to hear and understand what is heard. This is commonly referred to as having a "good ear." This might be hearing intervals or chord changes or listening to music and being able to transcribe what you hear. Trained auditory skill enables you to recognize patterns by ear and then play those patterns.

Rhythmic: The ability to "feel" music and groove. Having a sense of time and being able to embody a pulse.

Creative: Putting it all together—the technical, mental, rhythmic, and auditory—in an immediate setting. Taking all aspects and developing them into new ideas by improvisation or exploring by writing music or new musical ideas.

Developing your musical relationship in all of these areas will help you to become the musician you are looking to be. Spend time on the things that come natural to you and definitely get some time in on the things that aren't so natural or don't come so easily.

Time

Making time to practice is essential to development, and I encourage carving out time each day to explore music. It's not about the actual hours spent; it's about the focused time spent. Short, attentive spurts can be far more effective than long sessions in which your mind wanders. I was once told that "we make time for the things that we value," and I believe we do, either consciously or subconsciously. If you look at how you spend your time, it will show you what you value in life. Making time for the things we enjoy and are curious about enriches our lives and helps to give us meaning, purpose, and excitement.

Practicing the Blues

Blues, like any form of music, has developed over time. If you are looking for a raw, emotional kind of blues artist, or if you prefer a more technical performer, the blues has it. Practicing can help you develop in any of the areas that you wish; there is no correct way to go about it. If you are having a problem with anything in music or the blues, you can explore it from different angles, and that is what this lesson is about. Another thing to consider: When making the time to practice, having a direction or goal is really helpful. If you want to get somewhere in music or any type of skill, having a direction in mind helps you organize what it is that you'll be practicing and working on. Spend time envisioning what you'd like to have happen in regard to music and the blues. It instills emotions, and emotions are the fuel that drives our actions in life.

Rhythm, an essential ingredient of music, is the movement or timing of events. As humans, we recognize patterns in everything. In music, we recognize melodic and rhythmic patterns. It's these patterns, or motifs, that have us singing or dancing. Rhythmic motifs are the repetitive, recurring patterns in a song, such as the groove, the melody, or a solo. In this lesson, we'll explore some rhythmic motifs that you can use while soloing to help create continuity and memorable lines for the listener to connect with.

Motif

In music, a motif is a repetitive, recognizable succession of notes. Using a motif is a great way to build a solo or create melodies. It also helps the listener follow along.

I started playing the blues in my early 20s. At that time, I was really into playing technically. When I'd be on the bandstand and it was time for a bass solo, I'd play the blues like a young kid who just drank 10 cups of coffee. Needless to say, the only people who noticed the bass solo were my fellow musicians, and the only thing I was saying to them was the Mixolydian scale—really fast. I noticed this problem early on and realized that, in order to capture the audience and for me to connect to the music, I had to slow down and play some motifs. I had to play memorable rhythms and melodies, not a bunch of scales! I wasn't playing the blues; I was playing the scales in a blues song. A huge difference.

Let's start with some simple rhythmic motifs over a C7 chord.

EXAMPLE 1

This first example is 16 bars of C7. It's for you to practice different motifs over. Skip it for now and come back when you've finished the lesson.

EXAMPLE 2

In this next example, a rhythmic motif is established with the root note. As the example progresses, the rhythm stays the same but different notes are introduced.

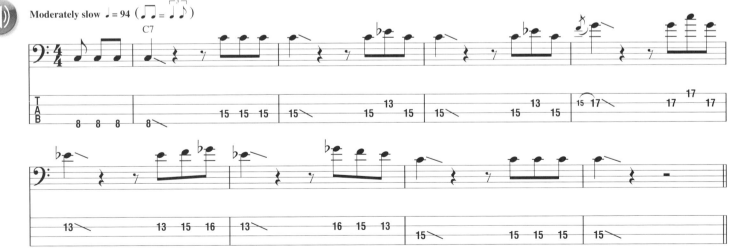

That is a great way to start a solo. If the example continued, different rhythmic figures could be added to the motif or the motif itself could be abandoned altogether and a new motif could be started. The possibilities are endless.

For the next few examples, a two-bar rhythmic motif is established with the root note (C) and then followed by bass improvisation using the motif so you can hear how each one can be developed. After you become familiar with each motif, go back to Example 1 and use the audio track to practice it yourself.

EXAMPLE 3

EXAMPLE 4

EXAMPLE 5

EXAMPLE 6

LESSON #39: MELODIC MOTIFS

Melody is a series of musical notes that form a musical structure or idea. It is built by combining pitch and rhythm. Melodic motifs are combinations of pitch and rhythm that seem to tell a story within the music by catching the ear of the listener. These repetitive melodic motifs are the melodic building blocks that we hear in songs. In this lesson, we'll explore some melodic motifs for building solo ideas.

Making Melodies

Melodies are repetitive, recognizable musical phrases. Look at the current mainstream music scene or the common commercial on television and you'll recognize the power of melody. I'm sure that you've had the experience of not being able to eradicate a melody or song from your head when you want it to be gone. Conversely, it's wonderful when your favorite song sticks around in your head all day. When it comes to playing the blues, melody is a powerful force as well. It's the difference between a good song and a bad one. When soloing or playing lines, melody is the hook that captures the listener, and when those melodies are backed by emotion, it transforms a room.

EXAMPLE 1

This first example is 16 bars of C7. It can be used as a backing track for you to practice over. Skip it for now, but come back as you progress through the lesson.

EXAMPLE 2

For this next example, a melody is played twice and then expanded upon with different notes and rhythms. Practice this melody over the audio from Example 1.

EXAMPLE 3

This example has a little more space. Notice the build at the end and the restatement of the melodic idea.

For the next two examples, a two-bar melodic motif is established and then followed by bass improvisation using the motif so you can hear how each one can be developed. After you become familiar with each motif, go back to Example 1 and use the audio track to practice it yourself.

EXAMPLE 4

EXAMPLE 5

The primary function of the bass is as a rhythm instrument. Many bassists stick to practicing all things rhythm, and that is great to do, but it is really helpful as a musician to practice melodies as well. Working on songwriting and soloing, or generally expanding your musicality, will help your bass playing. Practice playing along with melodies; it's great for your ear and your melodic expression.

LESSON #40: SLAP BASS: SLAP AND POP TECHNIQUE

Slap bass is an extremely popular technique for bass due to its rhythmic sound—it makes people want to get funky. The thumb slap mimics a kick drum and the finger pop mimics the snare drum, and because bass is a harmonic instrument, you get notes to go along with the slap and pop. Blues slap technique is primarily used for funky blues songs and for soloing. It's not very traditional, but it really can break things up in a set or when you want to get people on the dance floor.

Thumb Slap

The thumb slap is basically like it sounds: you slap the thumb against the string. To do this, make a loose fist and stick your thumb out like you're about to give the "thumbs up" sign. The movement to strike the string comes from a pivot of your wrist/ forearm, not your thumb. Keep your wrist loose and strike the intended string with the first joint of the thumb, allowing the string to bounce against the fretboard of your bass. The key to striking the string is to let it bounce, rather than have it rest on the string when you are done.

EXAMPLE 1

Let's practice the thumb slap. Take your time and let the note ring. Work towards achieving a percussive attack with the thumb. A thumb slap is notated with a "T" between the notation and tab staves.

EXAMPLE 2

Once you get comfortable with the movement, move on to this exercise. This is the first six bars of a 12-bar root shuffle in A.

EXAMPLE 3

Dead notes are really common in slap bass. To execute the mutes, lift your fretting hand slightly from the strings. Let's do a shuffle in G.

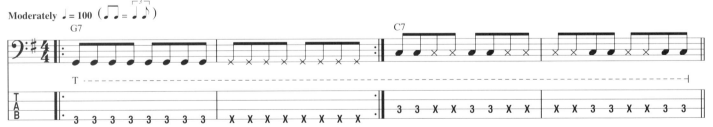

It's best to get comfortable with the thumb slap before moving onto the finger pop. The finger pop will come pretty easily if you can perform the thumb-slap technique fluidly, relaxed, and cleanly. Practice the thumb slap on all four strings and with all kinds of bass lines.

Finger Pop

The finger-pop technique involves snapping the string with one of your plucking fingers to create a popping sound. While you can use either your index or middle finger, most people use the index. The finger pop is basically an extension of the thumb slap—all you need to do is get your plucking hand ready. Loosen your index finger and create a hook. Place just enough of your finger under the string so as to grab it and then pull up just hard enough to make it snap or pop. To get the correct motion for the finger pop, combine it with the thumb, using one motion. The movement comes from the pivot of the forearm: thumb-slap down, finger-pop up. Finger pops are notated with a "P" between notation and tab staves.

EXAMPLE 4

Let's start with a dead-note exercise so we can concentrate exclusively on the plucking/popping hand. Mute the strings with your fretting hand.

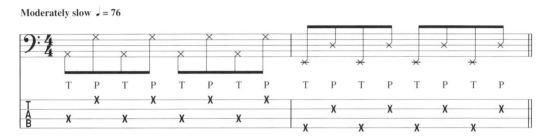

EXAMPLE 5

Now we'll add the notes. Keep the percussive slap and pop sounding nice and clear.

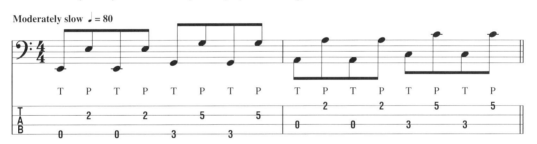

EXAMPLE 6

Here's an octave pattern in a shuffle feel.

SLAP BASS: 12-BAR GROOVES

Here are some 12-bar blues examples using the slap-bass technique. When playing slap bass in a blues context, remember: you are the glue that keeps things together, and if you are too busy and all over the place, the glue can come apart. Another thing to be aware of is your groove. Playing funk can be tight and right on or it can have a super laidback feel, almost like you are sliding into each note slightly behind the beat.

EXAMPLE 1

Here are some funk blues grooves that work really well with the slap-bass technique. This groove is great over slower funky blues.

Your Arsenal of Grooves

On the bandstand, you'll be asked to play all kinds of songs that you don't know, especially if you sit in or are a sub. You'll hear "this one's a funky blues in…" and it's your job to play some kind of funky bass riff in that key. Ready! 1, 2, 3, 4, go!

If you are familiar with a bunch of funky blues bass lines, you can pick from your arsenal of grooves and go; if you don't have an arsenal, you can draw from the songs that you've heard from listening to the blues. Occasionally, you might be asked to play a funky slap-bass part. In that case, adapting a bass part that you are familiar with or playing a slap groove that you already know works well. Being familiar with different feels and standards in a genre is really helpful when creating bass lines and playing in a certain style.

EXAMPLE 2

This next groove is inspired by an Albert Collins song called "Bending Like a Willow Tree" and adapted for slap bass.

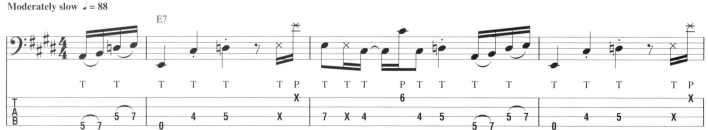

EXAMPLE 3

Here's another groove built from the root, 6th, and ♭7th. It's inspired by the Temptations' "Shakey Ground."

LESSON #42: 8-BAR BLUES

The 8-bar blues is another common form of the blues and is used in folk, rock, jazz, and of course, blues. The 8-bar blues is built from two four-bar sections. The first section is the statement and the second section is the response. The I, IV, and V chords are the usual suspects in an 8-bar blues, although several variations are used. Let's take a look at the 8-bar blues and some of the most common progressions.

Here is one of the most common progressions in an 8-bar blues. It's found in songs like "Key to the Highway" and "Trouble in Mind."

I7	V7	IV7	IV7
I7	V7	I7	V7

EXAMPLE 1

Here's that progression in the key of A.

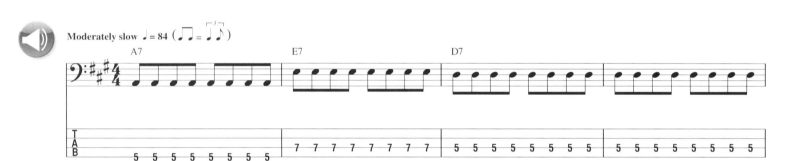

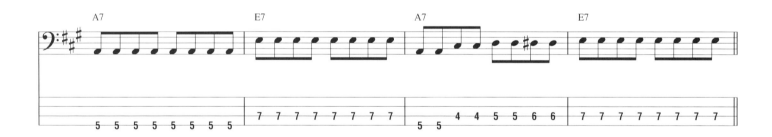

A I7–IV7 change can be substituted in bar 7.

This one's another common progression, as heard in songs like "Worried Life Blues."

I7	I7	IV7	IV7
I7	V7	I7–IV7	I7–V7

EXAMPLE 2

Let's try it in the key of C.

This next progression stays on the I chord for the first four bars and is found in the song "Heartbreak Hotel."

I	I	I	I7
IV7	IV7	V7	I

EXAMPLE 3

LESSON #43: FINGERSTYLE TECHNIQUE

Playing the blues all night long can be a workout, as it requires a steady and consistent plucking hand. Spending some time practicing plucking technique can make those shuffles sound rock solid and feel effortless. Let's take a look at several nuances that can make a huge difference in your playing.

Anchor

Playing box shuffles and walking lines require a lot of plucking-hand movement, and one of the major things to consider is the anchoring of your thumb. Basically, you have two options: anchor your thumb on the pickup while plucking the strings or move your thumb to different anchor points (the strings) when you pluck. When anchoring the thumb on the pickup, you have less movement and string muting mainly comes from your fretting hand. If your thumb floats and anchors on lower strings as you play the higher strings, the open strings are muted by your thumb as it moves and your movement is closer and less exaggerated.

Anchored on Pickup, Low

Anchored on Pickup, High

Floating Low

Floating High

Follow-Through

Having a consistent, even pluck is essential to having great tone and fluid technique. Keeping your plucking fingers close to the strings (not lifting them between plucks) helps your speed and accuracy. A technique that really helps keep your fingers consistent is something I call "follow-through." Pluck the string up towards your chest. After each pluck, the finger rests or follows through to land on the next, lower string. To work on follow-through, pluck the A string with your first finger and allow it to follow through and come to rest on the E string below. Do the same with your second finger and you'll notice that your fingers only move as far as the spacing between strings. Let's work on following through.

EXAMPLE 1

This exercise is in free time so you can get used to the movement before moving onto bass lines in tempo. Practice this really slow at first.

Free time

Alternate Fingers

When working on plucking, alternate each finger. If you use two fingers, make sure that you alternate between first and second finger with every pluck. If you use three fingers, alternate all three. Keep your plucking nice and tight. As soon as you pluck with the first finger, place your second finger on the string that you just plucked to stop it from ringing. Maintain this back-and-forth movement: pluck, mute, pluck. This will keep your fingers ready for action and close to the strings.

EXAMPLE 2

Slowly ♩ = 60

If you practice follow-though, you will notice that the finger that you just used is resting on the lower string, ready to play. If the next note is located on the lower string, you don't have to lift your fingers at all—just pluck.

EXAMPLE 3

Here is a bass line for practicing follow-through. Fingering patterns are written between the notation and tab staves.

Once this feels natural, speed up the pattern and add a shuffle feel!

LESSON #44: TRADING FOURS

Another way of adding some excitement to the end of the solo section is to trade fours. Trading fours is a form of soloing in which each member of the band takes four bars. This can happen amongst soloists, or it can happen as a round robin, with every musician taking four bars. Trading fours is also often used to give the drummer a solo by alternating the drums and other instruments every four bars.

Trading on a 12-Bar Blues

The challenge with trading fours is keeping your place in the form, especially if the band is alternating every other four bars with the drummer, because everyone stops for the drummer. It's important to keep the changes in your head while these stops occur so you can come in at the right place in the form, at the right time. Being that a 12-bar blues is made up of three four-bar sections, the top of the song comes around every three soloists. Let's take a look.

EXAMPLE 1

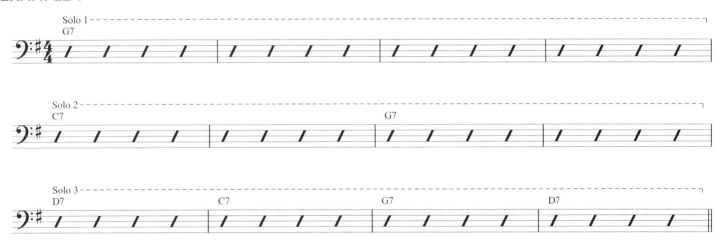

If you are alternating with the drummer every four bars, keep in mind that the form will be drummer on solos 1 and 3 the 1st time, then drummer on solo 2 the second time through the form. Also keep in mind that the drummer won't be playing over the same changes every time, nor will the other soloists, so it's really important that you know where you are in the form. Let's take a look at the layout with drums alternating every four bars.

EXAMPLE 2

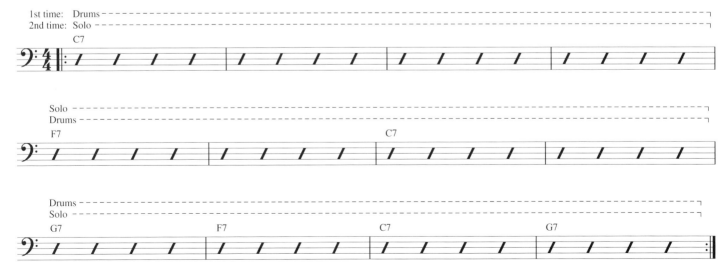

Let's play a blues with the drums trading fours. Hit the downbeat at the beginning of each drum solo. The drummer will take the second solo the first time through and the first and third solos on the repeat.

EXAMPLE 3

Trading

Trading solo measures isn't limited to four bars; it's normal to trade other lengths as well. Sometimes you might trade an entire 12-bar blues or just two bars. If you are playing other forms of music like an 8-, 16-, or 32-bar form, you might trade eight-bar solos. The key in any of these scenarios is to keep your place and support the soloists and—oh, yeah—don't forget to take your own solo!

LESSON #45: JAZZ-BLUES BASS LINES

Jazz-blues bass lines are walking parts that have a bit more freedom than standard walking blues parts. This is partially due to jazz-blues changes being more complex, which creates more harmonic movement for the bassist to walk within and less repetition for common themes to be present. In this lesson, we'll explore some common jazz-blues chord progressions and look at walking bass parts that work over these changes.

Basic Jazz-Blues

The basic form for a jazz-blues starts out like a regular blues, with a quick change in bar 2. At bar 9, a ii7 chord is added, moving to the V7 in bar 10, and in bar 12, a quick ii7–V7 is added to bring you back to the top.

I7	IV7	I7	I7
IV7	IV7	I7	I7
ii7	V7	I7	ii7–V7

Jazz-blues bass lines follow the traditional walking rules found in swing blues but aren't tied to any specific patterns other than walking through the changes.

EXAMPLE 1

Count Basie Blues Changes

Count Basie blues changes are named after William "Count" Basie, an American jazz pianist. The progression features a ♯iv° chord in bars 2 and 6, both following the IV7 chord, and a vm7–I7 in bar 4, followed by a ii7–V7 in bars 9–10.

I7	IV7–♯iv°	I7	vm7–I7
IV7	♯iv°	I7	VI7
iim7	V7	I7	I7

EXAMPLE 2

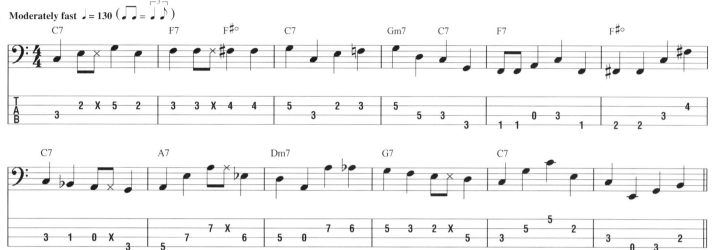

Moderately fast ♩ = 130

Bebop Changes

This common jazz-blues form adds a few more chord changes to the mix, including a iiim7–VI7 change in bar 8 and a iiim7–VI7–iim7–V7 turnaround in bars 11–12.

I7	IV7	I7	vm7–I7
IV7	♯iv°	I7	iiim7–VI7
iim7	V7	iiim7–VI7	iim7–V7

EXAMPLE 3

This example has chord slashes and an audio track for you to practice playing over.

Fast ♩ = 150

C7   F7   C7   Gm7   C7

F7   F♯°   C7   Em7   A7

Dm7   G7   Em7   A7   Dm7   G7

LESSON #46: FILLS: THE WALK-UP

Bass fills in blues are great for adding anticipation prior to a chord change, for building movement during a section, or to just add some color in different parts of a song. The walk-up is a fill that is used to anticipate or forecast the next chord change. It creates rhythmic and harmonic movement via an upward walk. Let's look at some common walk-ups.

Walking Up to the IV Chord

EXAMPLE 1

Here's a root shuffle in G. In bar 4, the walk-up maintains the rhythmic motif, although it could be played with quarter notes.

EXAMPLE 2

Here's a box-shape shuffle in G. This example uses a quarter-note walk-up in bar 4.

EXAMPLE 3

Here is a nice, groovin' blues in the key of C. For this type of feel, we use the same rhythm in the walk-up but change the last two notes.

EXAMPLE 4

Here's a walking shuffle in the key of G. Again, a standard quarter-note walk-up is used.

EXAMPLE 5

Walk-ups can be quicker as well. Although quick walk-ups don't add as much build-up to the IV chord, it's nice to change things up on occasion. This next example uses a box-shape pattern in the key of A and a quarter-note walk-up on beat 4.

EXAMPLE 6

Here is the same example, but with an eighth-note triplet on beat 4.

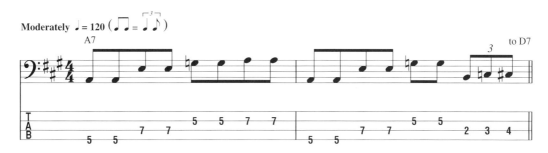

Walking Up to the V Chord

Here are some examples that walk up to the V chord.

EXAMPLE 7

This is a typical walk-up to the V chord in the key of A.

EXAMPLE 8

Here is a box-shape shuffle with a similar walk-up.

Walking Up to the I Chord

You can also walk up to the I chord from the IV chord with the same walk-up motifs used in this lesson. For example, in the key of G, you can use a one-bar walk-up from the C7 in bar 6 by using quarter notes—C, E, F, and F#—to resolve to the I chord, G7.

LESSON #47: FILLS: THE WALK-DOWN

Just like walking up, the walk-down creates a sense of movement for the listener—almost like a forecast of things to come. Let's take a look at some walk-downs.

Walking Down to the IV Chord

EXAMPLE 1

Here is an example of a walking shuffle in the key of F. In the measure before the IV chord, switch direction and walk down.

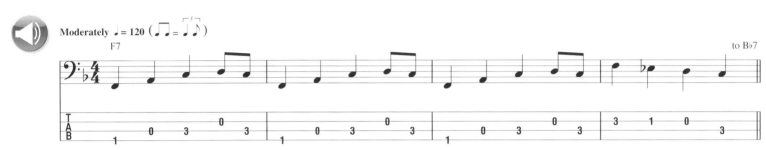

EXAMPLE 2

For this box-shape shuffle, stay on the octave and walk down to the IV chord in bar 4.

EXAMPLE 3

Walk-downs sound great in a slow blues. The bass breaks from the bass line and starts a walk-down, which tells the listener that a change is about to occur.

EXAMPLE 4

This example is a shuffle with a descending bass line, which segues to a walk-down (bar 4) to the IV chord.

Walking Down to the I Chord

This next section contains several walk-downs from the IV chord to the I chord.

EXAMPLE 5

Here is an example of a chromatic walk-down from the IV chord, starting on the ♭7th (beat 2).

EXAMPLE 6

This one has the same walk-down but is played with a box-shape shuffle groove.

EXAMPLE 7

Here is the same box-shape shuffle, but with a triplet walk-down to the I chord on beat 4.

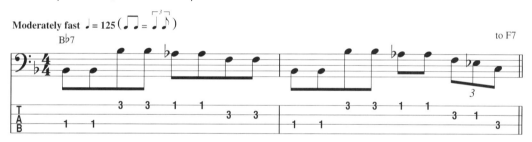

Walking Down to the V Chord

EXAMPLE 8

This one is a 12/8 blues in G. It starts at bar 7 of a 12-bar blues and walks down to the V chord.

EXAMPLE 9

Here is the same 12/8 blues. Instead of landing on a descending, chromatic passing tone before the V chord, land on the root of the IV chord, C, on beat 4 and ascend to the V chord. Technically, it's a walk-down with a one-note walk-up.

LESSON #48: OTHER FILLS

In the blues bass idiom, many bass parts are similar or similarly structured. What makes a blues bassist sound different? How can you achieve your own sound? Your groove and sound have everything to do with your personal voice. The things you add to standard parts and how you add those nuances are another way to personalize that sound. There are plenty of ways to improvise a fill and add different character to a standard fill. In this lesson we'll take a look at how to use technique, different note choices, and different rhythms to add character to a fill.

Technique

Adding different techniques like dead notes, grace notes, slides, hammer-ons, and pull-offs lends a unique sound to the fills that you play. The following are ways to add some of that spice to your fills. Just keep in mind that adding too much spice can make a meal hard to eat, while just the right amount adds a great flavor.

Let's take a standard walk-up and add some different techniques. All of these examples are played in the key of G and at the same tempo with a walk-up to the IV chord.

EXAMPLE 1

This example adds some dead notes on the off-beats of the walk-up. Dead notes can add extra rhythm to a fill without adding any notes that might clash.

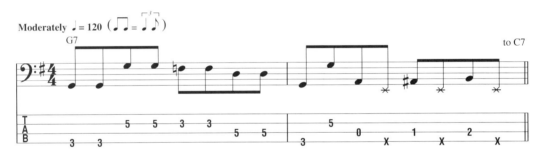

EXAMPLE 2

This is an example of using several dead notes to really push the rhythm.

EXAMPLE 3

In this walk-up, slides are used to add a more legato feel to the line.

Melodic and Rhythmic Ideas

Adding melodic and rhythmic fills between chord changes can add some interest by anticipating the change, as well as adding a unique flavor. Like the previous figures, all of the following examples are played in the key of G and at the same tempo.

EXAMPLE 4

Here is a more melodic example of a fill using slides and a pull-off.

EXAMPLE 5

This example adds a triplet pull-off and incorporates the ♭5th.

EXAMPLE 6

For this one, some triplets are added to give liftoff before the IV chord.

EXAMPLE 7

Sometimes keeping it simple by playing octaves can really fill the space and make the line sound big. Allow the notes to ring fully.

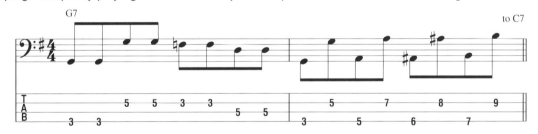

EXAMPLE 8

This example adds a faster triplet fill. Fast lines can build intensity and are great for ramping things up.

These examples are templates for you to explore your own musical voice. It's perfectly fine to stay with the standard blues fills, but it's also nice to add some of your own ideas. It's really up to you and may depend on the gig you are playing.

LESSON #49: SOLOING OVER THE I CHORD

Occasionally, the bassist gets a chance to solo in blues. This can be a welcome opportunity for some, and an aversion for others. Usually, the fear comes from not having experience soloing or not having enough confidence. Like anything in life, taking time to explore or practice something helps to build skill, and after those skills develop over time, you can put those skills into action. Taking a solo is a great chance to express yourself and a great opportunity to take a break from your usual role and step into new territory. In this lesson, we'll explore some concepts related to soloing over the I chord.

Getting Started

EXAMPLE 1

Here are 16 bars of C7 for you to play over. Move on to the other examples in this lesson but come back to this backing track when you're ready to test drive the ideas in the other examples.

We'll be starting with the C blues scale.

C Blues Scale (Moveable Shape)

3fr

EXAMPLE 2

Let's start by playing freely within the C blues scale over the I chord. Try walking quarter notes over the I chord and then double the note values (i.e., play eighth notes). It's not important to have a killer solo; just get familiar with moving around the scale using swung eighth notes. Listen to the audio track to get an idea of what to do and then try it yourself.

EXAMPLE 3

Now start to break up the rhythm. Listen to the audio track and then go back and try it.

Moving Forward

When soloing, here are some tips:

▶ Transcribe a melody and incorporate it into your solo.

▶ Start with a rhythmic motif and build from that.

▶ Start with a melodic motif and build from that.

▶ Pick different scales and practice making melodies from the notes.

▶ Transcribe different licks and mix them into your solo.

▶ Work out different techniques and add them to your solo.

Scales

Below are some scales that you can use to play over the I chord (C7 in this case).

C Blues Scale

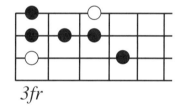

3fr

C Major Pentatonic

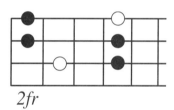

2fr

C Minor Pentatonic

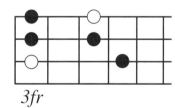

3fr

C Mixolydian Mode

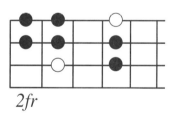

2fr

C Composite Blues Scale

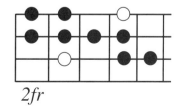

2fr

LESSON #50: SOLOING OVER THE IV AND V CHORDS

The blues is a style of music that is built from three chords: the I, the IV, and the V. These chords are usually dominant in quality. Despite their dominant quality, however, the sound is still based on a major tonality. In this lesson, we'll look at some common scale options for soloing over a C blues. These examples can then be transferred to any key.

EXAMPLE 1

Before we start looking at the IV and V chords, let's look at a 12-bar blues in the key of C. This audio track will be a template for you to practice the scale options over. As you learn each scale, you can come back to this track and practice.

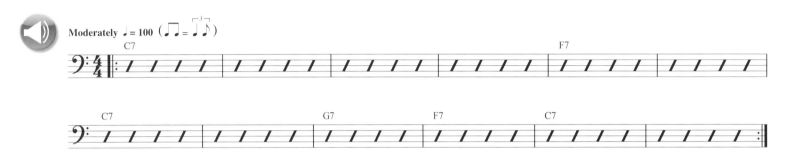

The IV (F7) Chord

The great thing when soloing over the IV chord is that you don't have to switch scales. You can, but you don't have to. The scales that work over an entire blues progression are the blues scale and the minor pentatonic scale, both in root position.

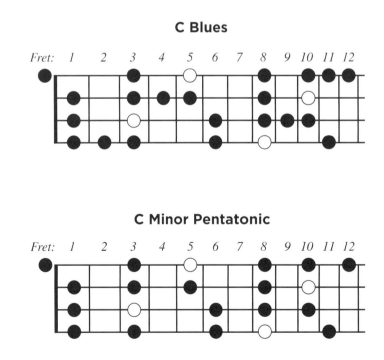

When using the C blues and C minor pentatonic scales over the IV chord, the ♭3rd of the scale, E♭, functions as the ♭7th of the IV (F7) chord.

Another option when going to the IV chord is to switch scales and play F Mixolydian. The scale's B♭ and D notes add a bit of a jazzier flavor.

F Mixolydian

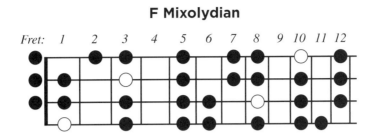

Take some time and practice running through Example 1's audio track with the C blues scale and the C minor pentatonic scale. Try to create melodies out of the notes in the scale. Next, try using F Mixolydian over the IV chord, especially in bars 5–6.

The V (G7) Chord

When soloing over the V chord, you can use the C blues and C minor pentatonic scales just like you did over the IV chord. Another scale that works well is C major pentatonic. It sounds happier and contains the note D, which is the 5th of the G chord. There are several other options for the V chord that sound great as well. Let's take a look.

G Blues

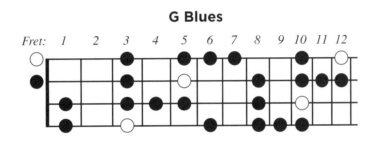

G Minor Pentatonic

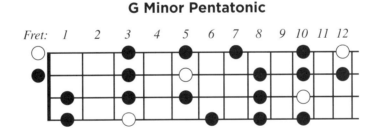

G Mixolydian

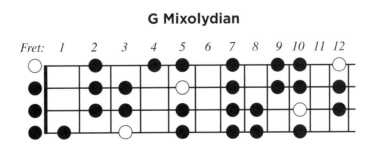

Go back to Example 1's audio track and play these scale options over the V chord so you can familiarize yourself with the sound of each scale. Take your time and work out different melodies with each scale. Also, listen to blues soloists and see if you can figure out what kind of note choices the players you really like are making.

LESSON #51: ARTICULATION

Articulation refers to whether notes are legato (smooth and connected) or staccato (short and clipped). In legato phrases, we hold each note for its full rhythmic duration and try to leave as little gap between notes as possible. When playing staccato, the notes are clipped short of their full rhythmic value—often by half or more.

The two approaches yield vastly different results, which is a good thing when you're looking for variety while playing the same material over and over. Whereas legato sounds flowing, calm, and even, staccato sounds abrupt, aggressive, and edgy. Both certainly have their place, and the well-rounded bassist will exploit both in his/her playing.

Of course, I'm not suggesting that you freely choose either to use at any time. There are certain styles of blues in which one or the other is certainly more common. For example, in slow blues, legato playing is much more common than staccato. In fact, you'd be hard-pressed to find someone playing staccato bass lines in a slow blues. With funkier styles, you're much more likely to hear some staccato playing. In shuffles, you'll hear a mixture of both to great effect.

Let's check out some examples to hear the effect of varying articulations. We'll start with a typical shuffle pattern in G that you've heard a thousand times.

EXAMPLE 1

First, here's how it would look and sound if played legato.

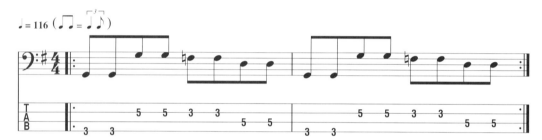

EXAMPLE 2

Now let's check out the same line played staccato. The dots on each notehead indicate that they're to be played staccato.

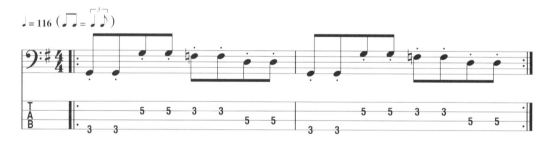

Notice that it sounds like an entirely different groove. It sounds tighter and more focused.

Let's take a look at another example.

EXAMPLE 3

This one's a funky line in D. First, here's the legato version.

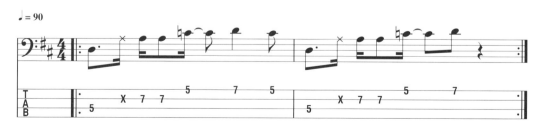

EXAMPLE 4

And now here's the same line performed staccato.

Again, it sounds almost like a different line. But all of the notes are the same; the only thing different is their duration.

Playing staccato is often an intuitive thing, but it still takes a bit of practice. It's easiest when you're playing fretted notes exclusively. You simply pluck the note and then quickly release pressure with your fretting finger to kill the note.

Pluck note

Release fret-hand pressure

With open strings though, it's a bit more difficult. You have two choices: you can stop the string with your plucking hand or with a fret-hand finger. If you're just pedaling on the open A string in eighth notes, for example, it's easy to stop the string with your plucking hand, because you're going to pluck the same string again anyway. You simply plant the finger on the string a bit earlier.

For example, let's say you wanted to play the shuffle pattern from Example 1 in the key of A and in open position. That would look like this:

EXAMPLE 5

That gets a little trickier. When moving quickly from string 3 to string 1 like that, it's harder to stop string 3 on the "and" of beat 1. It can be done, but you'll probably find it easier to use your fret hand to quickly mute string 3 just before you fret string 1 for the high A note. So, if you were going to fret the A note on string 1 with your first finger, you could have it "at the ready" while your other fingers reach over to string 3 and mute it just before the high A is plucked.

Blues music simply has to groove in order to be effective, and as the bass player, you make up half of the mighty rhythm section that churns it out. Therefore, it's vital that you remain prepared to lay it down thick. There are certain fretboard patterns that grow ripe, groovy veggies for the plucking, and some people call these "groove boxes."

The Low Down

A groove box is basically a fretboard area in which many commonly played lines can be accessed with relative ease. When you're on the gig, you don't want to have to worry about fingerings or shifts when you're trying to groove. Once you become familiar with these groove boxes, you'll be armed with several options that will serve you well—no matter which direction you decide to take the groove.

Groove Box #1: First Finger on Fourth-String Root

Groove Box #1 is by far the most common. This box plants your first finger on the fourth-string root and is based around the two-fret octave shape. In the key of G, it would look like this:

The cool thing about this box is that you can handle almost all the notes with your first and fourth (or, if you prefer a little stretch, third) fingers. With this shape, you've got several key grooving notes at your disposal. Here are some of the most important:

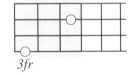

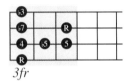

In this box live some of the most common groove lines of all. Here's a typical example in G:

EXAMPLE 1

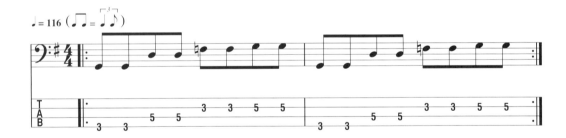

Or you could also play a straight-eighths groove in this vein using this box.

EXAMPLE 2

Groove Box #2: Second Finger on Fourth-String Root

Groove Box #2 is really common for walking bass lines. It puts your second finger on the fourth-string root and basically extends Groove Box #1 by one fret. Here's how it looks in the key of G:

This box gives us access to all the notes in Groove Box #1 and adds the all-important 3rd and 6th tones.

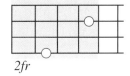

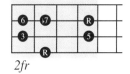

This is where the classic boogie line lives.

EXAMPLE 3

But you can also play some great funky stuff in this box as well. Here's a line that demonstrates this in C, which puts us in seventh position:

EXAMPLE 4

Groove Box #3: Fourth Finger on Third- or Fourth-String Root

Groove Box #3 can be based off either a fourth-string root or a third-string root. So, depending on what key you're in, your fourth finger will handle the root on one of these strings.

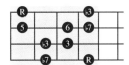
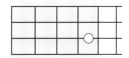

The big benefit of this groove box is the nice, low notes below the root.

EXAMPLE 5

Here's a typical line to demonstrate that idea. This one's in D minor, with a third-string root.

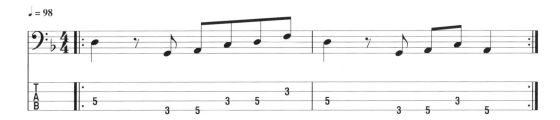

Get these groove boxes under your fingers, and you'll never be too far away from a deep groove!

LESSON #53: OCTAVE DISPLACEMENT

As a blues bassist, you'll play countless shuffles, slow blues, and straight-eighths blues. While there's something to be said for "practice makes perfect," playing the same thing over and over *and over* again can become a bit of a strain on your sanity. Therefore, anything we can think of to keep things fresh is welcomed in my book. One idea in this regard is octave displacement.

Octave displacement simply refers to the act of moving a note, or set of notes, up or down an octave to inject new life into a repeated bass line. It's a simple tool that, once mastered, can make it seem as though you're playing much more elaborate lines than you really are. In other words, it can make the ordinary sound… well, less ordinary!

How It Works

The idea is pretty simple, really, although it can seem a little elusive at first. Basically, you look at a line and try to find a spot in which you could jump an octave in a musical way. Explanation by example is probably best here. Let's take a look at a typical walking line in D.

EXAMPLE 1

Now here's what it sounds like if we keep the first note where it is but move the rest of the line down an octave.

EXAMPLE 2

Obviously, you'll need to reposition your fret hand so that your fourth finger is on the D note, but it gives the line a completely new weight and feel.

Here's another take on this line. What if we change only one note? Here, we'll move the root note up an octave the second time through but keep the rest of the line where it is.

EXAMPLE 3

Here's a straight-eighths groove idea in G minor that takes this idea to the extreme. First, we move up an octave and then down an octave. You may not want to go this far with the idea very often, but it demonstrates that things like this are a possibility.

EXAMPLE 4

This type of thing doesn't always have to be a literal transposition either. You can take the same idea and transpose it, perhaps using a slightly different rhythm but with a clearly identifiable relationship at work. Here's an example of that kind of thing with a funky line in E. Notice that the B–D–E motive in the upper register is varied slightly in the lower octave, but the connection is clear.

EXAMPLE 5

As you can see, this isn't rocket science. But a well-placed octave displacement can really open up a line and keep things from getting too stale. The next time you find yourself repeating a line that you've played a hundred times, give this idea a try and see if you can come up with something new.

METRONOME TRICKS FOR IMPROVIN' YOUR GROOVIN'

There's simply no better practice for improving your time than practicing with a metronome. For beginner or intermediate players that have never played with one, the first time is normally a painful eye-opener. Playing to a click in the studio is the same thing, obviously, and in the old days, many players unfortunately found out how bad their time was after already having booked time in an expensive studio. These days, most players have the means to record themselves, so that scenario is less common. Nevertheless, the metronome still reigns supreme for time-keeping.

No matter how much you practice with one though, there are still some habits that you can develop that might sneak under the radar. Most of these deal with what happens *between* the clicks. In this lesson, we'll take a look at some metronome tricks to help make sure that your entire beat—not just the downbeat—is in good shape.

Cut It in Half and Turn It Around

One of the most common ideas—especially in the jazz world—is to set the metronome to half time. In other words, instead of clicking on every beat, it will click on every other beat; specifically, beats 2 and 4 (the backbeats). By doing this alone—with no music playing—the beat seems to swing a bit.

EXAMPLE 1

Obviously, the slower you set the metronome, the more difficult this becomes, as there is more space to evenly traverse between the clicks. Faster speeds eventually get difficult, too. The results are well worth it, though, so push yourself!

Turn It Up!

Nope, this is not a metronome exercise for playing Skynyrd tunes. This means we're going to place the click on the upbeat. So, instead of the metronome clicking on beats 1, 2, 3, and 4, it'll be clicking on the "and" of those beats. If you tap your foot on the beat, the upbeat occurs when your toe is up off the floor.

EXAMPLE 2

This is kind of like the double-time version of the first idea, but it doesn't really feel that way because of the straight eighth notes. This exercise gets harder the faster you go.

One Step to the Side

The first two examples were child's play compared to this next exercise but, holy moly, does it help even out your 16th notes! The idea here is to play a funky 16th-based line and have the click land on either the "ee" or the "uh" of the beat; that is, either the second 16th note ("ee") or the fourth one ("uh"). If you've never tried this before, it's very difficult at first to even hear the click this way, much less play along to it. No pain, no gain though!

EXAMPLE 3

EXAMPLE 4

Another idea is to have the metronome click on both the "ee" and the "uh" of the beat. If you have a metronome that allows you to do this (some do), just set it up that way. Otherwise, simply set it twice as fast as you had it for the previous examples. In other words, if you were playing at 90 bpm with it clicking on the "ee," then set the metronome for 180 bpm for it to click on the "ee" and the "uh."

EXAMPLE 5

These 16th-based ideas can feel very disorienting at first, but once you get solid with them, playing with a click on beat 1 will feel like child's play in comparison. Good luck!

LESSON #55: TRIAD ARPEGGIOS

If there's one bass style in which learning your arpeggios is of paramount importance, it's the blues. The lines that we play in the blues are *heavily* based on arpeggios of all kinds, and the more fingerings for them you know, the better you'll be equipped to improvise something new or to just freshen up a dusty old line. In this lesson, we'll be looking at triad arpeggios.

Though we'll use major triad arpeggios far more often than minor ones—and much more than augmented or diminished—we'll look at each type for the sake of being thorough. Who knows? You may be on a gig where a chart with augmented chords gets thrown at you, and then you'll thank me!

Here are the most common triad shapes. In all of these grids, the root is shown as an open (white) circle. This is critical because, without knowing where the root is located, these shapes will do you no good. The root is your "north star," so keep your eye on it at all times. The shapes that comprise only three strings can be shifted up a string set as well.

Major (1–3–5)

Root Position (Root on Bottom)

First Inversion (3rd on Bottom)

Second Inversion (5th on Bottom)

Minor (1–♭3–5)

Root Position (Root on Bottom)

First Inversion (3rd on Bottom)

Second Inversion (5th on Bottom)

Augmented (1–3–♯5)

Notice the symmetry in the augmented fingerings. The augmented chord consists of stacked major 3rd intervals.

Root Position (Root on Bottom)

First Inversion (3rd on Bottom)

Second Inversion (5th on Bottom)

Diminished (1–♭3–♭5)

Root Position (Root on Bottom)

First Inversion (3rd on Bottom)

Second Inversion (5th on Bottom)

Pick a root note—C, for example—and work through all of these shapes for that root. You can try working through them all from a different root each day, eventually covering all 12 roots. Some of these shapes will certainly fall under the fingers better than others, so feel free to experiment with them to see what feels most comfortable. Once you get these shapes down, you'll be quite surprised at how much the neck will open up to you.

Arpeggios make up a huge portion of bass lines in blues, so it only makes sense to know as many fingerings for them as you can. The more options you have, the freer you'll be when constructing your lines or improvising them on the spot. In this lesson, we'll look at seventh-chord arpeggios. Although the dominant seventh chord reigns supreme in blues, we'll also look at a few other chord types that you'll definitely come across from time to time—especially in jazzier blues styles.

Here are the most common seventh-chord shapes. In all of these grids, the root is shown as an open (white) circle. This is critical because, without knowing where the root is located, these shapes will do you no good. The shapes that comprise only three strings can be shifted up a string set as well.

Dominant Seventh (1–3–5–♭7)

Root Position (Root on Bottom)

First Inversion (3rd on Bottom)

Second Inversion (5th on Bottom)

Third Inversion (7th on Bottom)

Minor Seventh (1–♭3–5–♭7)

Root Position (Root on Bottom)

First Inversion (3rd on Bottom)

Second Inversion (5th on Bottom)

Third Inversion (7th on Bottom)

Major Seventh (1–3–5–7)

Root Position (Root on Bottom)

First Inversion (3rd on Bottom)

Second Inversion (5th on Bottom)

Third Inversion (7th on Bottom)

Pick a root note—C, for example—and work through all of these shapes for that root. You can try working through them all from a different root each day, eventually covering all 12 roots. Some of these shapes are more comfortable than others for sure, but it's best to work through them all—even the less-practical ones—because they'll improve your fretboard knowledge immensely. With a solid command of these shapes, you'll feel much less constrained in your playing and will gain considerable confidence in branching out from your well-entrenched fretboard trails.

LESSON #57: CHORD THEORY: TRIADS

As bassists, we can sometimes get by without knowing much in the way of chord theory. After all, a good percentage of what we play is root notes, and we often learn to fill in the bits in between by mimicking what we've heard in bass lines from our favorite recordings. But you're doing yourself a great disservice if you neglect to learn some chord theory. This isn't the sexiest topic, but you'll be much better prepared to improvise bass lines, vary the ones you know, and even compose your own lines or riffs, upon which you can base a song. In this lesson, we'll look at the triad and what makes it tick.

The Basics

A triad is so named because it contains three different notes: a root, a 3rd, and a 5th. These numbers are referring to intervals as measured from the root note. There are two parts to an interval: a quantity and a quality. The quantity is the easy part; it just involves counting note names. If C is the root note, for example, we'll call that "1." Therefore, if we count up from C, we'll get E as the 3rd and G as the 5th.

C (1) – D (2) – **E (3)** – F (4) – **G (5)**

So a C triad, regardless of what type, will contain some kind of C, E, and G notes. However, there are four different types of triads that we can create with variations of these three notes: major, minor, augmented, and diminished. And that's where the interval quality comes in. The quality is determined by the number of half steps that the interval spans.

For example, from C to D is a 2nd. We know that because only two note names are involved: C (1) and D (2). More specifically, C to D is a major 2nd because it contains two half steps: C to C♯ (first half step) and C♯ to D (second half step). From C to D♭ is a minor 2nd because it contains only one half step. So the number (2nd) tells us the quantity, and the first word (major, minor, etc.) tells us the quality.

Interval Names

So, how do we know that two half steps is a major 2nd? Well, you just have to memorize it. But there's logic to it. If we analyze all 12 of the intervals from a C root note (until we reach the octave C), this is what we'll come up with:

Notes	# of Half Steps	Interval Name (and abbreviation)
C to C	0	Perfect Unison (P1)
C to D♭	1	Minor 2nd (m2)
C to D	2	Major 2nd (M2)
C to E♭	3	Minor 3rd (m3)
C to E	4	Major 3rd (M3)
C to F	5	Perfect 4th (P4)
C to F♯	6	Augmented 4th (A4)
C to G♭	6	Diminished 5th (d5)
C to G	7	Perfect 5th (P5)
C to A♭	8	Minor 6th (m6)
C to A	9	Major 6th (M6)
C to B♭	10	Minor 7th (m7)
C to B	11	Major 7th (M7)
C to C	12	Perfect Octave (P8)

Let's look at a few of the apparent truths that we can deduce from the above table:

▶ The qualities of major (M) and minor (m) apply to 2nds, 3rds, 6ths, and 7ths.

▶ The quality of perfect (P) applies to unisons, 4ths, 5ths, and octaves.

▶ A minor interval is one half step smaller than its major companion. In other words, C to D is a M2, but C to D♭ is a m2; C to E is a M3, but C to E♭ is a m3, etc.

▶ A diminished interval is one half step smaller than its perfect-interval companion. In other words, C to G is a P5, but C to G♭ is a d5.

▶ An augmented interval is one half step greater than its perfect-interval companion. In other words, C to F is a P4, but C to F♯ is an A4.

Triad Construction

So now that we know something about intervals, let's see how this applies to the four triad types. Earlier, I stated that a triad contains a root, 3rd, and 5th, and therefore a C triad would contain some kind of C, E, and G notes. Now that you know the intervals, you can add them to these notes.

▶ From C to E is a major 3rd

▶ From C to G is a perfect 5th

MAJOR

The major triad is kind of the standard, in that it doesn't require any alteration to the numbers. If you just see a "C" chord symbol, it implies a C major triad, whose numeric formula is: 1–3–5. This is a shortcut to avoid having to say "root, major 3rd, perfect 5th" all the time.

MINOR

The minor triad also contains a perfect 5th, but instead of a major 3rd, it contains—you guessed it—a minor 3rd. Makes sense, doesn't it? A minor triad's numeric formula is: 1♭3–5. The only thing different from the major triad is the 3rd, which has been lowered by a half step (flatted).

AUGMENTED

An augmented triad is like a major triad in that is has a major 3rd, but the perfect 5th has been replaced by an augmented 5th. Therefore, its numeric formula is: 1–3–♯5.

DIMINISHED

In a diminished triad, we have a minor 3rd (like the minor triad), but the perfect 5th has been replaced by—can you guess?—a diminished 5th. Its numeric formula is: 1♭3♭5.

And there you have it. That's the way triads are built. Once you get familiar with this lesson, be sure to build triads from different root notes. Remember to count letter names for the interval quantity and half steps for the quality! Good luck!

CHORD THEORY: SEVENTH CHORDS

Seeing as blues music is built almost entirely on dominant seventh chords, it only makes sense to have a pretty good grasp on them. However, many players—and not just blues musicians—couldn't tell a dominant seventh chord from a minor seventh flat five on paper. Although you obviously don't have to be able to read music or know theory to be a great player, it can only improve your musicianship—not to mention your marketability as a player. Chances are, if you ask a great player who doesn't read music, they'll tell you they wish they could.

In this lesson, we'll look at the construction of seventh chords. Though the dominant seventh chord is by far the most common type in blues, we'll take a look at several types. If you're playing a jazzier blues style, you'll definitely come across more than just dominant chords, and minor blues often makes use of others as well. Due to space constraints, we'll have to assume some basic knowledge up front. If you're starting from scratch in the theory department, you should probably get a handle on scales and triads before digging in here.

Basic Review

To review, let's talk quickly about the construction of the triad, as it's the foundation upon which the seventh chord is built. The triad consists of a root, 3rd, and 5th. In the case of a C triad (or C major, specifically), this means C, E, and G: **C (1, or root)**– D (2)–**E (3)**–F (4)–**G (5)**. There are four types of triads that we can create with the root, 3rd, and 5th:

> **Major:** root, major 3rd, perfect 5th (1–3–5)

> **Minor:** root, minor 3rd, perfect 5th (1–♭3–5)

> **Augmented:** root, major 3rd, augmented (sharp) 5th (1–3–♯5)

> **Diminished:** root, minor 3rd, diminished (flat) 5th (1–♭3–♭5)

In the key of C, here's what those would look like:

Obviously, major and minor triads are by far the most common of this bunch. But it's important to be familiar with them all, because you never know when they'll pop up on a chart somewhere. And unless you want to be stuck playing nothing but the root note when that happens, you need to know how they're built.

Adding the 7th

Once you understand triads, building a seventh chord is not that difficult. Basically, you add the 7th interval on top to create a four-note chord. Depending on which type of 3rd (major or minor), 5th (perfect, augmented, or diminished), and 7th (major or minor) you use, you create different types of seventh chords.

DOMINANT SEVENTH

This is by far the most common chord in blues. Also referred to as simply a "seventh chord" (e.g., C7), the dominant seventh is like a major triad with a minor 7th interval on top. Its numeric formula is: 1–3–5–♭7.

MINOR SEVENTH

A minor seventh chord (Cm7) is like a minor triad with a minor 7th interval on top. The numeric formula is: 1–♭3–5–♭7. You'll often find these in minor blues forms.

MAJOR SEVENTH

A major seventh chord (Cmaj7) consists of a major triad with a major 7th interval on top. Its numeric formula is: 1–3–5–7. Major seventh chords will often appear as the ♭VI chord in a minor blues, and they'll appear in some jazzier blues styles as well.

MINOR SEVENTH FLAT FIVE

This chord is like a diminished triad with a minor 7th interval on top. You'll see these chords in some jazzier blues as well. The numeric formula is: 1–♭3–♭5–♭7.

Now that you understand how to construct these seventh chords, try building them from roots other than C. If you get stuck, remember that the intervallic formulas are there to help you. If you need a refresher on the number of half steps in a certain interval, you can find charts easily on the web. Good luck!

EVERYONE NEEDS TO GET ON THE SAME PAGE!

If you've been to more than a few open-mic blues jams, you've more than likely seen or heard your share of musical train wrecks. These can range from something as small as one beat to something as large as a full-on derailment. Occasionally, this may happen because one of the players happens to be spacing out, trying to order a beer from the stage, or trying to make eye contact with that attractive someone sitting at the front table. More likely, though, these train wrecks occur from a simple lack of communication between the players.

The following is a list of factors that need to be agreed upon before the count-off. Though it's not impossible, it's much more difficult to discuss things while you're playing due to the volume, the fact that the guitar player won't open his eyes for you to get his attention, etc. So just get these things straight before y'all kick off a tune. This is of utmost importance if you're playing a song that not everyone knows!

> ## ALWAYS ASSUME THE RESPONSIBILITY IF NO ONE ELSE DOES!
>
> Unless you're playing a song that has a clear, established intro and/or outro that everyone knows, these should be discussed. As we'll see, this can be as brief as someone yelling "from the V!" Or it can be a bit more detailed. If no one else steps up and takes charge in this regard—and everyone is just standing around, waiting for someone to count it off—it's up to you to take the responsibility and establish what will be done! Do *not* assume everyone will play the same thing. Chances are, if it's not a well-known song with an established intro, you could be headed for a train wreck.

The "Same Page" List

THE INTRO

There are numerous well-established intros to blues tunes. Among some of the most common are:

> ▶ **From the I Chord (from the top):** This is as simple as it gets. The drummer counts off a four count and everyone hits the downbeat at the top of the form.

> ▶ **From the Turnaround (shuffle):** In this intro, you start from measure 11 of the form and run through the turnaround. You'll be moving from the I chord to the V chord. If the guitarist is going to be playing a chromatic turnaround lick on guitar, you may want to establish which one (ascending or descending) to play.

> ▶ **From the Turnaround (slow blues):** This will still start from the same point, but the turnaround in slow blues tunes is usually different than those in shuffles; it normally moves as follows: I (two beats), IV (two beats), I (two beats), and V (two beats).

> ▶ **From the V Chord (measure 9):** In this intro, you're starting from measure 9 in the 12-bar blues form. So we'll be playing a measure of V, a measure of IV, and then the two-measure turnaround. This one's especially popular in slow blues.

That covers probably over 95 percent of the intros that you'll encounter. A common train wreck on intros involves one person starting from the V chord and someone else (who didn't get the memo) starting from the I chord. Here's how that sounds.

The lesson: make sure *everyone* gets the memo!

QUICK CHANGE OR SLOW CHANGE

This refers to measure 2 of the 12-bar form. Are you going to move to the IV chord in measure 2 or are you going to remain on the I chord for measures 1–4? Listen to what happens when the guitar moves to the IV chord and the bass stays on the I chord. It doesn't sound so hot!

SOLOS/DYNAMICS

Try to get a sense of when everyone is going to take their solo. It'll help you be prepared to change your line if you choose to do so. Also, if the soloist wants to dramatically drop the volume for his second solo, for example, it's nice to know those kinds of things ahead of time. And of course, it would greatly help to know if you're going to be asked to solo!

STOPS/ENSEMBLE HITS

A common move in blues is for everyone to hit the downbeat and stop, letting the vocalist sing a line by him/herself. You can hear this type of thing in "I'm Tore Down" and "Pride and Joy," to name a few. What happens when you're not prepared for this type of thing? You end up looking… kind of silly.

TEMPO/FEEL CHANGES

Some songs, like "Hideaway" for example, feature shifts from a shuffle feel to a straight feel or vice versa. Be sure that you know if anything like that is in store, otherwise you might hear something like the accompanying audio example.

OUTROS

Outros, outros, outros… This is the No. 1 spot where you're likely to hear a train wreck at a blues jam. Everyone gets going on the tune, thinking they all know it, but they don't think about when or how they're going to end it. Often, it's not discussed, unless it's a very specific ending, but the standard blues ending—a turnaround with a chromatic ♭II–I change, or sometimes a VII–I move at the end instead of the V chord—always applies unless otherwise indicated. Listening and paying attention here is critical, because you have to be ready at the drop of a hat. The guitarist/harmonica player/etc. could do something as slight as throwing his/her hand up a beat or two before they want the band to stop for his/her outro lick, and you have to be ready.

So what happens when half the band thinks the song is ending and the other half doesn't agree? Listen and find out. You'll probably recognize this train wreck!

Summary

The most important thing at a gig is to sound great while the music is playing. If you're nailing the songs when you play them, no one is ever going to fire you from a gig for asking too many questions. So, if you're playing with a new set of people, save yourself some trouble and get clear on the important things up front. Your audience will thank you, even if the rest of the band takes it for granted!

The blues is an interesting style in that it's so well-established in many respects, but it's also incredibly improvisatory in others. For this reason, it's easy for strangers to get together and sound good the first time they play together, but it's difficult to sound *excellent*. The secret here is good communication between the players while playing. As a member of the rhythm section, we don't have the luxury of closing our eyes and losing ourselves in the music the way the soloists do. Our job is (most often) to support them and make them sound even better. And the best way we can do that is by paying attention.

Different Types of Cues

There are several different ways a musician (singer, guitarist, harmonica player, etc.) may try to communicate with you during a performance. While some of these will seem clearer than others, you need to do your best to figure them all out.

1. HAND IN THE AIR AT THE END OF THE SONG

A typical blues setting may have a few verses up front, a solo in the middle, another verse or two, and then another solo to end it. In this instance, it will end the same way probably over 75 percent of the time: the band will stop on the downbeat of measure 11, the soloist will bring it home with a final lick, and the band will join in for the final two chromatic chords (♭II–I or VII–I). To signal this ending, the soloist (often a harmonica player) will often throw his hand in the air a beat or two before this point, and you need to be ready for it.

2. GUITARIST RAISING HIS GUITAR NECK AND COMING DOWN ON THE BEAT

This is another variation on #1. If the guitarist is playing right before the hit, he'll often look back to the rhythm section and raise his guitar neck, indicating that the band is to stop on the next downbeat for his final lick.

3. PUSHING DOWN OR "SHUSHING"

Occasionally, a soloist will want to bring the dynamics way down for a solo (or during the middle of one). This will usually be conveyed with a palm moving down toward the ground or the "shushing" gesture (finger perpendicular to the lips). Or, if your guitarist is anything like Albert King was, he may just yell "turn that s--t down!" to the band.

4. BOUNCING, STANDING ON TOES, OR WIDENING EYES

Conversely, sometimes the soloist will want to wake up or rile up the band when they want to really cut loose. They'll often try to communicate this by bouncing on the beat, gradually getting higher with each bounce. They may also stand on their tip toes and/or widen their eyes.

5. GOING AROUND AGAIN

If the song is nearing the end but the soloist wants to make sure the band gives him another chorus, he might hold his hand up and twirl his finger in the air to signal "I'm going again."

6. DRUMMER RAISING STICKS FOR THE FINAL HIT OF THE SONG

This one's pretty self-explanatory, but you do need to be watching for it to go smoothly. If there's been some extraneous rumbling/soloing after the final chord, the drummer will most likely try to make eye contact with everyone before making the *final* final hit, so don't be the one that makes him wait five or 10 seconds to do it!

7. THE POINT

You'll most likely see this aimed at other members, but when the bandleader wants someone else to solo, he'll usually point at them. If he does point at you, however, you want to be ready, so be sure to have some nice licks stored in your bag of tricks!

This may not be a comprehensive list, as many of these kinds of things happen spontaneously, but it's a good start. The most important thing is to listen, look, and remain plugged in to what's going on. It feels really great when the band improvises something together as one unit, but that can only happen if everyone is in tune with each other.

LESSON #61: CHART-READING ESSENTIALS

If you don't know how to read a chord chart or a lead sheet, I highly suggest you learn how, as it will greatly increase your marketability as a player. In this lesson, we'll take a look at the essentials of chart-reading that every bassists needs to know.

Tempo/Style Marking

This is your first hint as to what type of song this is. Is it an uptempo shuffle, a slow blues, or a mid-tempo funky blues? Most charts will at least provide some type of direction in this regard by way of a tempo marking. Some charts will contain specific metronome markings (in beats per minute), while others will just use generic terms like "fast," "moderate," etc.

Key Signature and Time Signature

Next up is the key signature and time signature. These two bits of information also speak volumes about the song.

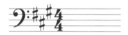

The key signature—a collection of sharps or flats—tells you the key of the song. A blank signature indicates the key of C (or A minor). All others will be a flat key or sharp key. Key signatures are something you just need to memorize, but you'll definitely notice patterns with how they work. Here are all 12 major key signatures and their corresponding relative minors.

Major Key	Relative Minor Key	Key Signature
C	Am	Blank
G	Em	F♯
D	Bm	F♯, C♯
A	F♯m	F♯, C♯, G♯
E	C♯m	F♯, C♯, G♯, D♯
B	G♯m	F♯, C♯, G♯, D♯, A♯
F♯	D♯m	F♯, C♯, G♯, D♯, A♯, E♯
F	Dm	B♭
B♭	Gm	B♭, E♭
E♭	Cm	B♭, E♭, A♭
A♭	Fm	B♭, E♭, A♭, D♭
D♭	B♭m	B♭, E♭, A♭, D♭, G♭
G♭	E♭m	B♭, E♭, A♭, D♭, G♭, C♭

If you're on the ball, you may have counted 13 key signatures in the chart above. That's not an error; it's just that one of them was listed two different ways. F♯ and G♭ are the same key; they're just different versions of one another. Either way, it's six accidentals, so pick your poison: sharps or flats!

The time signature is the set of stacked numbers that immediately follows the key signature. It tells you how the music is counted. The top number indicates how many beats are in each measure, while the bottom number indicates which type of rhythm is counted as one beat. The most common time signature is 4/4, and it tells us that there are four beats (4) in a measure and the quarter note (4) gets the beat. In fact, 4/4 is so common that occasionally you'll see a "C" in place of the time signature. This stands for "common," which means 4/4.

In 3/4, there are three beats (3) in a measure, and the quarter note (4) gets the beat. In 6/8, there are six beats (6) in a measure, and the eighth note (8) gets the beat. And so on. 12/8 is the most common time signature for slow blues.

Repeat Signs

A repeat sign is a shorthand way of telling you to repeat all the music that precedes that sign. Sometimes there are beginning ‖: and ending :‖ repeat signs; other times, there will just be an ending sign. In the former case, you repeat all the music enclosed by the two. In the latter, you simply repeat from the beginning of the song.

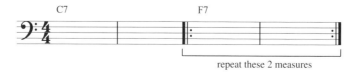

repeat these 2 measures

Sometimes you'll see a bracket with a number extending to (or from) a repeat sign. This is a simple way to tell the performer to repeat most of the music, but change the ending. The first time through, you play to the ending repeat sign (under the "1" bracket) and then go back to the beginning (or to the beginning repeat sign). The second time, you skip over the "1" bracket (first ending) and go directly to the "2" bracket (second ending) and continue on.

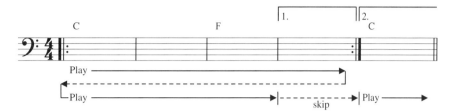

Rhythm Slashes

If you don't have a specific bass part written out, you'll often see a set of rhythm slashes. This simply tells you to improvise an appropriate part relative to the chord symbols.

If the composer wants you to play a specific rhythm, he/she will often indicate it in the chart with a slash/chord symbol combination. For example, the following tells you to improvise a line based on C7 for beats 1–3. On beat 4, however, you need to hit a G note along with the rest of the band for the G7 chord and sustain it through beat 1 of the next measure.

Routing Directions

The real space-saving devices in a chart are the routing directions. Before the days of music notation software, composers must have loved these. Routing directions appear toward the end of a song and can tell you several different things: go back to the beginning, go back to a specific spot, etc. They're all written in Italian terms, so you'll need to memorize them. Here are the most common directions and their meaning:

D.C. (Da Capo, Italian for "from the head"): Go back to the beginning of the song.

D.S. (Del Segno): Go back to "the sign," which is the s-looking symbol with dots (𝄋).

Coda ⊕: This crosshair-looking symbol signifies the beginning of the coda (Italian for "tail"), which is (usually) the last section of a song.

D.C. al Coda: Go back to the beginning, play until you see the "To Coda" sign, and then skip to the coda.

D.S. al Coda: Go back to the sign, play until you see the "To Coda" sign, and then skip to the coda.

So, in this example:

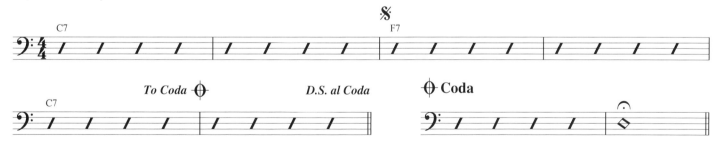

This is what you would do:

1. Play from measure 1 through measure 6, where you see "D.S. al Coda."

2. Go back to the sign, which is at measure 3.

3. Play until you see "To Coda," which is at the end of measure 5.

4. Skip to the Coda and play until the end.

By the way, the semicircle with a dot (⌢) over the final, whole-note chord slash is called a fermata. It tells you to sustain the note indefinitely.

UNDERSTANDING CHORD SYMBOLS

In this lesson, we'll look at the most common chord symbols, how they're notated, and what they mean. For the sake of consistency, we'll look at each one with a root note of C. By the end of the lesson, you should have a firm grasp on how to handle just about any chord symbol that you're likely to come across at your next gig.

Triads

Triads are built with only three notes, but they come in various configurations. The classic triad is built with a root, some type of 3rd, and some type of 5th. There are four of these: major, minor, augmented, and diminished.

MAJOR—COMMON SYMBOLS: C, Cmaj

If you only see a letter (C), with nothing else, the chord is a major triad, which contains a root, major 3rd, and perfect 5th. C major is spelled: C–E–G. You may also see this notated as "Cmaj," though it's not nearly as common. Depending on the style and key of the song, you'd usually base your line off either the matching major scale or Mixolydian mode. The matching major pentatonic is always a safe bet as well.

MINOR—COMMON SYMBOLS: Cm, Cmi, C-

A minor triad contains a root, minor 3rd, and perfect 5th. C minor is spelled: C–Eb–G. You'll often see "Cm," "Cmi," or "C-." You can base your line off the matching minor scale or Dorian mode, depending on the context. The minor pentatonic scale is also a good source for lines.

AUGMENTED—COMMON SYMBOLS: C+, Caug

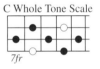

C Whole Tone Scale

The augmented triad contains a root, major 3rd, and augmented (raised) 5th. C+ is spelled: C–E–G#. This chord usually calls for the whole-tone scale, which is a six-note scale built exclusively from whole steps.

DIMINISHED—COMMON SYMBOLS: C°, Cdim

A diminished triad contains a root, minor 3rd, and diminished (flat) 5th. C° is spelled: C–Eb–Gb. The diminished triad is not nearly as common as the diminished or half-diminished seventh chord, but it does pop up occasionally. Oftentimes, someone will write a diminished triad when they really mean a fully diminished seventh chord (see below). If it truly is a diminished triad, it usually appears as the vii° chord of the key, in which case, you could simply use the notes of the parent major scale for your line. For example, if you see an F#° chord in the key of G, you use the G major scale for the fillers in your line, concentrating mostly on the notes of the F#° triad (F#–A–C).

In addition to those four, there are triads built from notes other than the root, 3rd, and 5th.

SUSPENDED 4TH—COMMON SYMBOLS: Csus4, Csus, C4

If you just see "Csus" on a chart, this usually means Csus4, which is the more specific notation. Csus4 is spelled: C–F–G. As we'll see below, there is another type of suspended triad, so when writing a chart, it's best to write "sus4" if that's what you want. This triad contains a root, perfect 4th, and perfect 5th. This type of chord is usually best handled with the root-and-5th approach, although other notes (such as the b7th) may work well too, depending on the context.

SUSPENDED 2ND—COMMON SYMBOLS: Csus2, C2

A suspended 2nd chord contains a root, major 2nd, and perfect 5th. Csus2 is spelled: C–D–G. Again, the root/5th approach works well with this chord. You may also see "C2" on a chart, but some people also use this symbol to mean an add9 or add2 (for our purposes, the same thing) chord. The big difference here is whether or not the 3rd is included. The 3rd is included for add9 chords, but not for sus2 chords. So, if you see "C2" on a chart, you may want to ask them which chord they mean. While it often sounds nice to play the major 3rd beneath an add9 chord (i.e., an inversion)—for example, playing E beneath a Cadd9—most composers will not want the 3rd played if they mean for the chord to be a "sus" chord.

SIXTH CHORD (MAJOR OR MINOR)—COMMON SYMBOLS: C6, Cadd6; Cm6, Cmi6, C-6

This chord is sometimes referred to as a triad, but not always. It can contain either the root, 3rd, 5th, and 6th or just the root, 3rd, and 6th. The only thing that differentiates major from minor is the 3rd—C6 = C–E–G–A (or just C–E–A), and Cm6 = C–Eb–G–A (or just C–Eb–A). The matching major scale, Mixolydian mode, or major pentatonic scale will work best for the major chords, whereas the matching Dorian mode or minor pentatonic scale will work best for the minor chords.

Seventh Chords

A seventh chord contains four different notes: a root, some type of 3rd, some type of 5th, and some type of 7th.

MAJOR SEVENTH—COMMON SYMBOLS: Cmaj7, CM7, C△

The major seventh chord contains a root, major 3rd, perfect 5th, and major 7th. Cmaj7 is spelled: C–E–G–B. In blues, you'll most often see the major seventh chord as the ♭VI chord in a minor blues. For example, you may see Cmaj7 in an E minor blues. Depending on the key of the song, either the matching major scale or the Lydian mode works well for this chord. For example, in the key of C, the C major scale would work nicely. In an Em blues, however, the C Lydian mode would usually sound nicer because it contains F♯, which is in the key of E minor (as opposed to F natural, which is not). Alternatively, the major pentatonic also works.

DOMINANT SEVENTH—COMMON SYMBOLS: C7, Cdom7

This chord contains a root, major 3rd, perfect 5th, and minor 7th. C7 is spelled: C–E–G–B♭. This is, of course, the most common chord in all of blues and is often used for all the chords (I, IV, and V) in a typical 12-bar shuffle. The matching Mixolydian mode is the de facto scale for this chord, but the major pentatonic can be used as well.

MINOR SEVENTH—COMMON SYMBOLS: Cm7, Cmi7, C–7

This chord contains a root, minor 3rd, perfect 5th, and minor 7th. Cm7 is spelled: C–E♭–G–B♭. Depending on the key and context, the matching minor scale or Dorian mode works well. The minor pentatonic scale is always a good choice as well.

MINOR SEVENTH FLAT FIFTH—COMMON SYMBOLS: Cm7♭5, C⌀, C–7♭5, Cmi7♭5

C Locrian Mode
8fr

Also referred to as a "half-diminished" chord, the minor seventh flat five contains a root, minor 3rd, diminished (flat) 5th, and minor 7th. Cm7♭5 is spelled: C–E♭–G♭–B♭. You'll occasionally run across these in jazzier blues styles. The matching Locrian mode usually works well on this chord.

FULLY DIMINISHED SEVENTH—COMMON SYMBOLS: C°7, Cdim7

C Diminished Scale
7fr

The fully diminished seventh chord contains a root, minor 3rd, diminished 5th, and diminished 7th (the same pitch as the major 6th). Technically, C°7 is spelled: C–E♭–G♭–B♭♭, but you'll usually see it spelled: C–E♭–G♭–A. You can also look at this chord as a series of stacked minor 3rd intervals. In that way, it's a symmetrical chord and therefore any of the notes can act as root. The matching scale for this chord is the diminished scale, which is an eight-note scale that alternates whole steps and half steps.

DOMINANT SEVENTH SHARP FIFTH—COMMON SYMBOLS: C7♯5, C+7

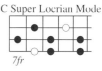
C Super Locrian Mode
7fr

This is an altered chord, the definition of which is a chord with an altered 5th or 9th (see below). You'll see these in jazzier blues settings. It contains a root, major 3rd, augmented (raised) 5th, and minor 7th. C7♯5 is spelled: C–E–G♯–B♭. This chord is handled by either the whole-tone scale (if a natural 9th is implied) or the super Locrian mode (if an altered 9th is implied, see below). The super Locrian mode is the seventh mode of melodic minor scale and is also known as the "altered scale."

DOMINANT SEVENTH SHARP (OR FLAT) NINTH—
COMMON SYMBOLS: C7♯9, C7♭9

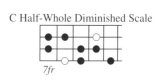
C Half-Whole Diminished Scale
7fr

Another altered chord—sometimes referred to as the "Hendrix chord" because of its famous use in "Purple Haze"—the dominant seventh sharp ninth contains a root, major 3rd, perfect 5th, minor 7th, and raised (or flat) 9th. (The 9th is the same note as the 2nd, only up an octave.) C7♯9 is spelled: C–E–G–B♭–D♯; C7♭9 is spelled: C–E–G–B♭–D♭. The matching half-whole diminished scale is used for this chord if a natural (perfect) 5th is implied, whereas the super Locrian mode is used if an altered 5th is implied. The half-whole diminished scale is like the diminished scale in that it alternates whole and half steps, but it starts with a half step, instead of a whole step.

That makes up the bulk of the chord symbols that you're likely to see on a blues chart. Get familiar with these scales and learn them in all keys and in several areas on the neck. If you do, you'll feel much more confident when you step behind that chart!

LESSON #63: SITTING IN THE POCKET

As a bass player, you're a firmly established member of the rhythm section. If you wanted to be flashy on your instrument, you would have played guitar, keys, saxophone, etc. But you chose to be one half of the formula that holds the whole band together (the drums being the other half, of course). As such, you have two main priorities: 1) playing the right notes, and 2) playing in time. This lesson focuses on the latter.

Pocket Talk

If you're in the rhythm section, the pocket is where you want to be. It's the most exclusive club in town, accessible to experienced, tasteful players that enjoy what they do—and do it well. It's what makes people's heads bob up and down, feet tap, and hips sway. It's the *groove*. When the rhythm section is in the pocket, the music feels deeper, heavier (not in a heavy metal kind of way), and more solid. It's hard to put into words, but boy, can you identify it when you hear it.

And that's your first assignment in this lesson: listen. And I mean *really* listen. Put on some old Motown or Stax record, press play, and just immerse yourself in the groove. Listen to the way the drums and bass interact with each other. Are they playing the same basic rhythms, or is the bass on its own, doing something unique? Listen critically and take note of any time you hear the bass player rushing or dragging. Chances are it won't be often, but you probably will hear it occasionally. After all, we're only human and many of those old records were made quickly, with the rhythm section knocking things out in one or two takes. The endless editing (nudging notes back and forth on the computer) available today wasn't available then, so they're not perfect—but they're damn good!

Off to the Races!

By far—and I mean by *far*—the most common culprit in playing is rushing. I'm not sure why, but we have a tendency to play ahead of the beat (sometimes by a crazy amount!) when we get nervous or when we're ill-prepared. We take it for granted now—you're nervous, so you rush—but when you really think about it, it's interesting that our bodies translate that feeling in that way. At any rate, it is what it is, and the only way around it is to become more prepared so that you're less nervous.

Think about it this way: let's say you're auditioning for B.B. King's band and you have to play (with B.B.!) four songs in different keys and rhythmic feels for your final test. If you do well, you get the gig. If you bomb, you can forget it. Would you be nervous? Probably so. However, what if the same audition required you to just play your open E string six times? How would you feel? Probably quite a bit better. Why? Because you've done that (played your open E string) thousands of times, and you feel 100% *prepared* to do it.

The Metronome Is Your Best Friend

It's really amazing how many musicians spend years (or perhaps their whole career) and never practice with a metronome (or a drum machine, which is another option). And you can normally spot them fairly quickly. They may have some chops and are able to pull off some impressive moves, but once you hear them groove, it becomes obvious who's spent time with the click and who hasn't.

The first time you play with the metronome, it's normally a shocking experience. (Hopefully, this first time isn't while you're playing along to a click track in a pro studio!) You can almost swear that the metronome is slowing down in the beginning. This is especially true when you try to play a complicated phrase or a speedy passage. But it's not. That thing just keeps on ticking like the Energizer Bunny. So lesson #2: get a metronome and use it… period! NO EXCUSES. If you want to be solid as a rock, you practice with a metronome. It's that simple.

Of course, playing with a drummer (and other instruments as well) is important. That should go without saying, as music is a cooperative art form. But what if your drummer doesn't have great time himself? Then it's not really helping your time. If you put four metronome-savvy musicians together to jam and then do the same with four who've never used one, the difference would be night and day. I guarantee it.

Examples

So let's listen to a few examples to hear all of this in action. You'll hear each example played twice. The first time, the bass will not be playing in the pocket; it will most likely be rushing, but it may drag a bit as well. The second time through, it will be sitting pretty. Nothing else (drums or guitar) will have changed at all.

 Moderate Shuffle in G

 Funky Blues in C

 Slow Blues in A

What did you think? It's quite a difference, huh? And this is just one instrument (the bass) messing with the groove. Imagine if you have several people playing out of time!

Summary

1. Listen, listen, listen! It's great to listen for pleasure, of course, but you should also spend some time listening critically to the pocket in your favorite recordings.

2. Get a metronome and use it. It's just that simple. It will literally be the best $10 you'll ever spend on your music career.

3. Listen critically when playing with others. Listen to the kick drum, the snare, etc. Are you locking in? If not, is it you or the drummer? The more prepared you are, the more you'll be sure of yourself when situations like that arise!

LESSON #64: YOU WON'T GET FAR ALONE

Practicing with a metronome is invaluable for any musician. In no better way can you get such immediate, hyper-critical feedback on your time. The metronome is your friend, yes, but he's your brutally honest one. He won't tell you that you look good in that shirt that's too short, and he'll have no problem telling you ladies that the dress does indeed make you look fat. But as helpful as the metronome can be, one cannot exist on a diet of metronome only; there's much more to playing music than playing in time, and that's what this lesson is about.

Music Is a Social Exercise

Playing music with people is a cooperative activity. No two musicians play the same material in the same way. Even if two drummers are playing the same exact beat, it won't sound exactly the same because no two people are alike. Because of this, when you play with different players, the music will feel different. Each person brings his own lifetime supply of experience, emotions, fears, and joys to their instrument every time they pick it up (or sit down with it). All of these things affect the musical outcome of any performance. The way you react to, bond with, argue with, or laugh with someone affects things as well. When you're happy, you'll play differently than when you're sad. In short, playing with other human beings is vital to your growth as a musician.

Different Ways to Skin a Cat

Let's take a look at a few musical examples to demonstrate how slight variations may affect what you play. This would be akin to playing with a different group of musicians or even playing with your drummer on a good night, bad night, happy night, or sad night.

EXAMPLE 1

Here's a moderate shuffle groove in C. The guitar sounds very heavy-handed in this groove, and that may result in you laying into it a bit more.

EXAMPLE 2

If the guitar player is playing something lighter and more buoyant, however, you may respond completely differently.

It's still a C7 chord, and it's still a moderate shuffle, but the feel and attitude has completely changed because of the choices of the musicians.

EXAMPLE 3

Let's take a look at a funky blues in D. The drummer here is playing a fairly busy pattern with lots of ghost notes and syncopation. As a result, you might tend to follow suit with a busier bass line.

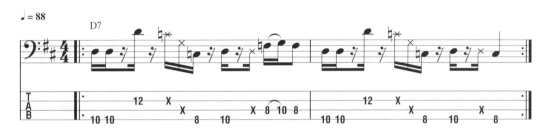

EXAMPLE 4

If the drummer were to reel it in a bit and play something simpler, it would certainly affect you. You might respond with something like this:

Summary

The point of this lesson is to demonstrate that what we choose to play is greatly affected by what others play. But, if you do nothing but sit in your practice room all the time, you're limiting your exposure to these different ideas. Some gigs may be routine, others may be fun or boring or aggravating. But others can be life-changing, and the same can even be said for jam sessions. Don't deprive yourself of these opportunities to grow and develop as a musician (and as a person!). In music, we can learn so much from others, and it often happens in ways we'd never think it would. But it won't happen at all if you don't get out there and do it!

PLAYING WITH THE KICK DRUM

As bassists, we often work in conjunction with the kick drum to derive our lines. Although this practice is somewhat less common in blues shuffles—as we tend to play on every quarter note (if not many of the eighth notes in between)—there are many other sub-genres of blues, such as funk blues and blues rock, in which this practice works extremely well. In this lesson, we'll take a look at how the kick-drum pattern can inform our bass choices.

Generally speaking, the basic kick-drum pattern is usually set up within the first two beats of a measure. This space normally defines the framework of the beat; that is, whether it will be more syncopated or straight, etc. So that's the most important place to examine when choosing your line. However, there are exceptions to this rule, as we'll see.

Funky Blues

Funkier styles generally translate to more rhythmically driven bass lines with less melodic movement. Often, either the snare drum or kick drum is syncopated, while the other remains fairly straight. Let's first check out a few examples in which the kick is playing straight while the snare is providing some syncopation. Notice the interesting juxtaposition caused by the bass following the kick even though the snare is highly syncopated in spots. Also realize that you don't have to play exactly what the kick drum plays. The idea is to use the kick drum to generate your line (i.e., not work against it), but you don't need to match it verbatim (although you can do that as well).

EXAMPLE 1

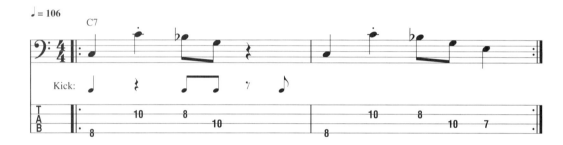

EXAMPLE 2

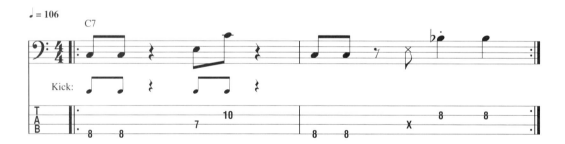

Now let's check out a couple of examples with syncopated kick-drum patterns, both of which are extremely common.

EXAMPLE 3

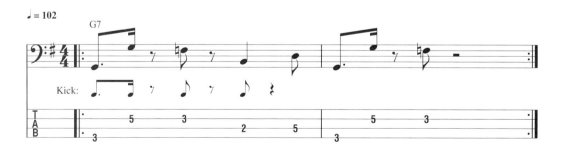

EXAMPLE 4

You can especially see in Example 4 how the kick really just serves as a guide when creating the bass line. We're playing many more notes than the kick, but we're making sure to accent the kick's rhythm as well.

Blues Rock

The blues-rock genre is basically a catch-all term that describes rock music with a decidedly bluesy edge. As such, there's quite a bit of music that can fall under this umbrella. Although 16th-note syncopation is not as common in this style, you will get some 16th-note kick patterns at slower tempos. Here's an example of that idea:

EXAMPLE 5

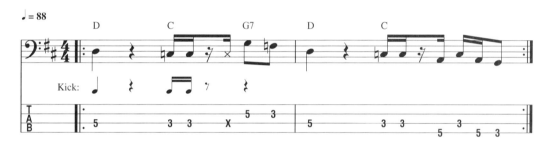

In many faster blues-rock songs, the guitar riff helps to drive the song as much as the rhythm section does. In this case, you can follow the guitar player while still paying attention to the kick drum, making sure that you're supporting its rhythm as well. Notice that, in the first measure, the kick drum plays on beat 1, but in subsequent measures, it's playing on the "and" of beat 4. As such, the bass (and guitar) follow suit.

EXAMPLE 6

Summary

The important take away here is to be sure to listen to what the drummer is doing. When the drums and bass complement each other, the result sounds bigger than the sum of its parts. If you're working against each other, though, you'll be greatly diminishing the strength of the groove. The kick drum should generally be your first checkpoint when charting your bass line, with the possible exception of some blues rock in which the guitar is the dominating force. But even then, the kick drum will usually be reinforcing the guitar's rhythm, so by aligning your line with either, you should be in good shape.

LESSON #66: KEEPING IT INTERESTING

Blues music is largely about subtlety. One typical complaint of listeners who aren't particularly big fans of blues is that a lot of it tends to sound the same. In fairness, it's easy to see why someone would say that. Many blues songs (not all, of course) share a great deal in common:

- ▶ They use the same basic 12-bar chord structure.

- ▶ They use the same basic vocal phrase structure (AAB).

- ▶ They often make use of the same melodic (i.e., minor pentatonic scale) and harmonic (dominant seventh chords) language, and so on.

Of course, to a fairly educated listener of the blues, it's easy to tell Muddy Waters from Howlin' Wolf, Albert King from B.B. King, etc. Once you become adept at listening for the subtleties, however, the same can be said for blues bassists, who tread a lot of the same ground repeatedly. In order to avoid becoming bored—and to keep things from sounding monotonous—it's nice to have a few ways to keep our job interesting. In this lesson, we'll look at several different ideas and strategies that can help you do just that.

You'll come across this type of pattern in a blues shuffle countless times. It's a staple of the language, and for good reason: it just sounds great.

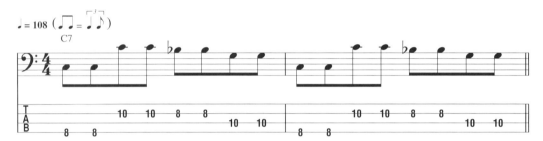

EXAMPLE 1

But the next time you're churning one of these songs, try mixing it up, perhaps when it's time for the guitar solo. Instead of descending from the top on beats 2–4, try ascending to the top, like this:

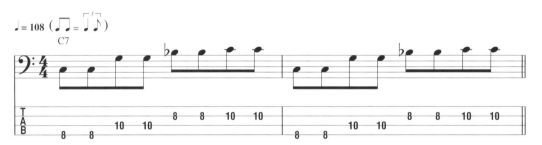

EXAMPLE 2

Or you could reverse the entire idea, starting from the top, going down the octave, and then coming back up.

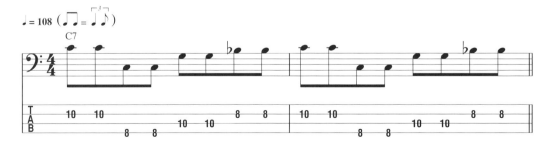

Or try another combination of those four notes. There are several more available!

When moving to a new chord, it's often nice to temporarily break from one of the aforementioned patterns. This is especially common when moving from the I chord in measure 4 to the IV chord in measure 5. The walk-up is a very common device. Here are two common variations on that idea:

EXAMPLE 3

EXAMPLE 4

EXAMPLE 5

Another nice, subtle idea when leading to the new chord is the simple addition of one chromatic passing/neighboring tone. For example, using the previous pattern, in measure 4 of a 12-bar shuffle in C, you could lead to the F chord with a simple, chromatic descent from the G like this:

EXAMPLE 6

Or when transitioning from the I chord in measure 8 to the V chord in measure 9, the exact same idea works as a chromatic lower-neighbor tone.

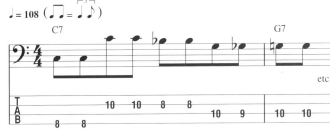

This idea is also great in a quarter note-based walking shuffle line. For example, here are two ideas for getting from the I chord in measure 4 to the IV chord in measure 5:

EXAMPLE 7

EXAMPLE 8

LESSON #67: MOVEABLE UTILITY PATTERNS

Though it's good to keep things fresh when playing the blues, given the limited vocabulary inherit in the genre, it's also imperative to have under your fingers plenty of patterns from which to draw in a moment's notice. With blues being an improvisatory style, anything can happen, and you need to be prepared. In this lesson, we're going to take a look at the moveable patterns that you need to have at the ready. They're not the flashiest things in the world, but they can really save the day when you're not thinking clearly for one reason or another. You can get by convincingly well by running some of these ideas on autopilot.

For the sake of simplicity, all of these patterns will be presented in the key of C, but be sure to practice them in all keys and all areas of the neck, as the fret distance will play a significant role in the comfort factor of these lines.

Dominant Seventh Boogie Patterns

EXAMPLE 1

This is as commonplace as they come, but if you don't know it, you can hardly even call yourself a blues bassist.

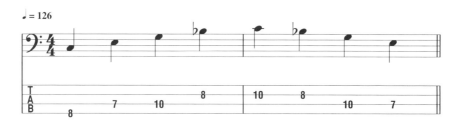

EXAMPLE 2

A common variation, this one employs the 6th and therefore only extends up to the ♭7th before walking back down.

Chicago Shuffle Patterns

EXAMPLE 3

Here's one of the most common eighth-note patterns of all.

EXAMPLE 4

A common variation, this one ascends instead of descending.

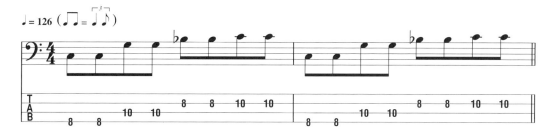

Constant Climb Patterns

EXAMPLE 5

In this pattern, you start with a high root and continually climb up to it. It's commonly played with the either the 6th or the ♭7th.

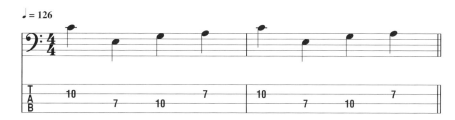

EXAMPLE 6

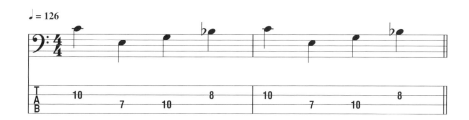

Treading Water Patterns

These patterns remind me of treading water because they don't cover a lot of ground. You're just kind of holding steady.

EXAMPLE 7

Here's a common descending one:

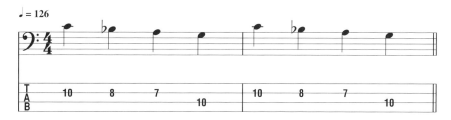

EXAMPLE 8

And here's one that's similar to the constant-climb pattern, only it uses half steps.

LESSON #68: ONE-CHORD SHUFFLE BLUES

In addition to the 12-bar and 8-bar blues, you'll occasionally come across the one-chord blues. These can be found in several variations, including the shuffle. Sometimes a song may consist entirely of nothing but one chord throughout, such as Howlin' Wolf's "Commit a Crime" (famously covered by Stevie Ray Vaughan, among others) and "Smokestack Lightnin." There may also be a song that contains a long verse (or other section) with only one chord, such as "Roadhouse Blues" by the Doors. This lesson, which applies to both types of scenarios, will look at a few strategies for handling this type of situation.

We'll stay in the key of E, which seems to be one of the most common keys with regard to one-chord blues. But you can transpose these ideas to any key.

Slow to Moderate Shuffles

Let's take a look at some different ways to handle slower or moderate shuffles, such as "Commit a Crime" or "Roadhouse Blues." Generally speaking, the slower the tempo, the more likely you'll feel inclined to incorporate eighth notes. But always feel free to experiment to see what feels best.

Standard Patterns

EXAMPLE 1

If there's not an established riff played by the guitars (or keyboards), you can always fall back on a typical shuffle pattern, such as this one:

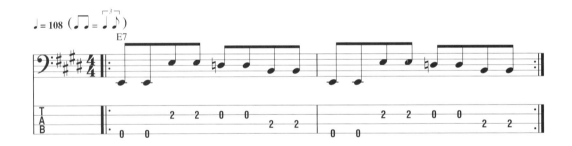

But there are nearly endless variations on this kind of idea. Basically, just about anything working with the root, 5th, and ♭7th tones (in this case, E, B, and D) is possible.

EXAMPLE 2

Here are several variations within these parameters:

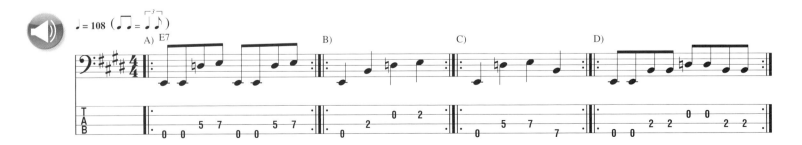

Ostinatos or Riffs

Or you can try more of an ostinato- or riff-type idea to mix it up. In this instance, you're acting more as a counterpoint to the other instruments, as opposed to a full-fledged bass line, but sometimes this can be just what a section needs. In this type of thing, the full minor pentatonic scale is often used. This adds the 4th (A) and ♭3rd (G) notes to the ones that we've been using. Try these ideas:

EXAMPLE 3

Uptempo Shuffles

For songs in the "Smokestack Lightnin'" vein, a cut-time bass line usually sounds great. Again, the root, 5th, and ♭7th notes often will be all you'll need.

EXAMPLE 4

Here are a couple of examples of this type of thing:

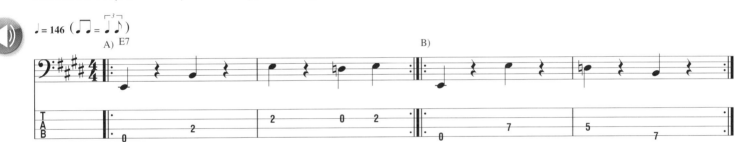

You can incorporate other notes from the minor pentatonic scale as well, depending on the context. If there are a lot of major 3rds being played or sung, you may not want to hang on the minor 3rd too much. But if it's all "in the cracks," then something like these ideas can sound great:

EXAMPLE 5

Summary

Even though it's counterintuitive, a one-chord blues doesn't have to be boring. Sure, you might end up playing the same thing over and over, but there's a certain excitement in that. You can really concentrate on just laying it down and getting lost in the groove. It can be a beautifully hypnotic and transcendent experience at times, and it feels great to be a part of something like that.

LESSON #69: ONE-CHORD BOOGIES

John Lee Hooker made a career out of them, and ZZ Top paid homage to him with what became one of their signature songs, "La Grange." We're talking about the boogie—specifically, the one-chord boogie. This is an uptempo groove with a swung-eighths feel and a driving rhythm. In this lesson, we'll take a closer look at this fun style and find out how we bass players fit into the puzzle.

The Basic Boogie

The basic idea of the boogie is to just vamp on one chord for six beats and then turn around on beats 3–4 of the second measure with two different bass notes. The chord often remains the same for these two beats (the I chord), but the bass notes help to create a sense of motion. For this lesson, we'll work in the key of A, which is the undisputed king of boogie keys, but you can transpose these ideas to any key.

EXAMPLE 1

Let's look at what is perhaps the most typical boogie line of all. This line moves to the ♭3rd and 4th to turn it around. In a more downhome style, the bass often plays quarter notes, like this:

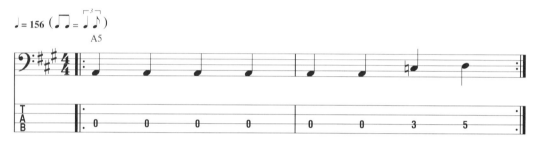

EXAMPLE 2

In more modern or high-energy boogies, however, it's not uncommon to move to eighth notes.

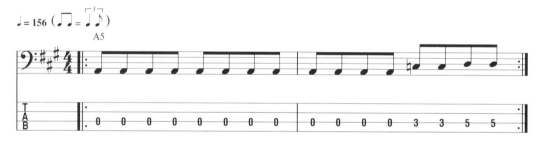

Variations

Now that you've got the basic idea, let's take a look at the myriad variations that you may encounter. It's important to be able to recognize them when you hear them, as these variations will often pop up spontaneously in an open-mic situation. For all of these variations, try them with both quarter notes and eighth notes.

EXAMPLE 3

Here's a common variation that simply replaces the 4th with the 5th (E).

EXAMPLE 4

In this one, we replace the 4th with the low ♭7th (G).

EXAMPLE 5

Another variation is to repeat the ♭3rd (C) twice.

EXAMPLE 6

Here's another idea that sounds great, because it gives it a low-register boost.

EXAMPLE 7

If you'd like to give the illusion of a bit of motion without really going anywhere, you can add a little walking line in measure 1, like this:

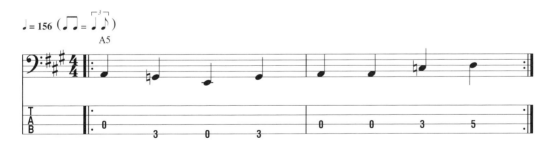

Summary

Though this lesson represents a good dose of the boogie lines that you're likely to encounter, there are plenty of other minor variations out there. But with these under you'll belt, you'll be prepared to handle a good 90 percent of them or so. Also, you can use variations to mix it up for a different "section" (if you can call it that in a one-chord boogie). Experiment with these ideas, listen to some of your favorite boogies, and have fun with it!

LESSON #70: ONE-CHORD SLOW BLUES

Ohhhhh, yeah. The one-chord slow blues is just about as downhome, lowdown as you can get. There's really one name that comes to mind when you think of this style: Muddy Waters. This isn't to say that many other blues artists haven't contributed to this lexicon, but the blues doesn't get much better than when Muddy kicks off "Mannish Boy" or "Hoochie Coochie Man." (While the latter isn't technically a one-chord blues, it does qualify here because it remains on the I-chord main riff for an extended period of time.)

In this lesson, we'll take a look at this style and examine some cornerstone riffs that you simply need to know. We'll also look at ways to generate a few well-placed fills, if you feel so inclined (I wouldn't overdo it!). So let's get low down.

The Basic Idea

Almost all one-chord slow blues share one thing in common: a pick-up riff, which occurs mostly on beat 4 (or technically, beats 10–12 of the 12/8 measure) before resolving to the tonic note on beat 1 of measure 1.

One-chord slow blues is especially interesting for the bass, because it often doesn't do what you think it does. By that I mean, on some of those old records, the bass isn't playing the same notes as the guitar/harmonica riff. However, many of these riffs are interchangeable, so it's not incredibly critical.

The Foundational Riffs

Here are a few foundational riffs that make up the bulk of what you'll hear on these kinds of tunes. For this lesson, we'll work in the key of A, but you can transpose these ideas to any key (though you may have to move up an octave at points).

EXAMPLE 1

Example 2 comes in two flavors. You'll probably run into both of them often.

EXAMPLE 2A

EXAMPLE 2B

EXAMPLE 3

EXAMPLE 4

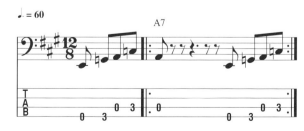

Variations on the Riff

Once the main riff is settled, there are a few common variations that you can employ, depending on what sounds best.

EXAMPLE 5

One of the most common variations is to continue to pedal on the tonic after the riff. Sometimes you'll hear this done in the form of one note per beat, like this:

EXAMPLE 6

But more often, the tonic will be played twice per beat, like this:

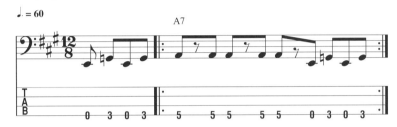

Fill Ideas

While it's often surprisingly fun to just lay back and repeat the same riff over and over—it just grooves that much!—you may also want to throw a well-placed fill in there occasionally. The scale of choice for this type of fill is almost always the minor pentatonic. In our case, that would be A minor pentatonic: A–C–D–E–G. Depending on whether you're playing in open position, third position, or fifth position, different scale forms may be used. More than likely, these four forms will suffice for most of your fill needs:

A Minor Pentatonic Scale

When inserting a fill, try to keep the following in mind:

▶ Try to keep it fairly simple, but if you're going to get a little fancy, do so at the beginning of the fill.

▶ End with a solid eighth note on a strong tone, such as the ♭3rd, ♭7th, or 5th—something that will lead nicely to the tonic.

▶ Keep these few and far between! The main riff is the train that drives the song.

EXAMPLE 7

Here are a few fill possibilities.

Almost everyone is familiar with the standard 12-bar blues form, and many players eventually become familiar with the jazz-blues form. But fewer know the Charlie Parker blues changes, also known as "Bird Blues." This is a highly modified form of the 12-bar blues that Charlie Parker used as a harmonic basis for songs like "Blues for Alice." It's got a lot of chords in it (we're not in I–IV–V land anymore, Toto!), and it can be pretty daunting if you don't understand what's going on. In this lesson, we'll break down the changes, take them apart, and put them back together so that you'll be prepared to handle the job, should it ever come up on a gig.

The Changes

In this lesson, we'll work in the key of C for the sake of simplicity, but be sure to run these changes in different keys once you get the hang of it. Here's what the basic Parker blues would look like in C:

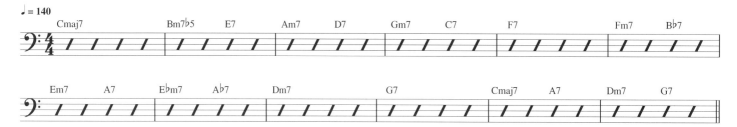

It should be noted that, in common practice, many of the dominant chords are altered. This is especially true of the E7 in measure 2 and the A7 in measure 11, both of which almost always appear with an altered 9th (e.g., E7♭9 and A7♭9).

Similarities

So, that's the basic idea. Like I said, Parker blues changes can look a little scary at first, but when you take them apart, they make much more sense. Let's take a look at everything that Parker blues changes have in common with the standard 12-bar blues and/or jazz-blues form.

▶ The I chord kicks off in measure 1. Granted, it's a major seventh chord here, but it's still the I chord in measure 1.

▶ We have a ii–V of IV (Gm7 to C7) in measure 4, which is exactly the same as the standard jazz-blues.

▶ The dominant IV (F7) chord appears in measure 5, just like a normal blues.

▶ Measures 9–12 are exactly the same as the standard jazz-blues, with the exception of the tonic chord, which is a major seventh instead of dominant.

So, we can see that, although many more chords are present, there are several checkpoints along the way that will feel familiar to us.

Differences

Now let's take a look at the measures that veer off the beaten path.

Measure 2 (Bm7♭5–E7): This is a ii–V of vi (Am7). The vi chord is a common substitute for the I chord, since they share three common notes: C, E, and G.

Measure 3 (Am7–D7): The Am7 here is the resolution chord of the previous ii–V (Bm7♭5–E7), and the D7 is the dominant (V) of the Gm7 chord that shows up in measure 4. So you could also say that the Am7–D7 is a ii–V of V (G), but the G shows up as a minor chord because it's functioning as a ii chord in the ii–V of IV progression of measure 4. You could also view measures 3–4, Am7–D7–Gm7–C7, as a iii–VI–ii–V of F (the IV chord).

Measures 6–8 (Fm7–B♭7, Em7–A7, E♭m7–A♭7): These three measures will sound much less exotic if you just get rid of the dominant chords and hold the minor seventh chords for the full measure. Then you have a simple, chromatically descending progression, Fm7–Em7–E♭m7, which leads to Dm7 (the ii chord) in measure 9. The dominant chords are simply the V chords of each minor-seventh ii chord. So each bar is a non-resolving ii–V progression: Fm7–B♭7 = ii–V of E♭, Em7–A7 = ii–V of D, and E♭m7–A♭7 = ii–V of D♭.

The good news is that all of these chord changes actually make our job a bit easier, if you can believe it. With so many changes happening so quickly, much of the guesswork is taken out. There are two basic approaches that you can take when creating your bass line, depending on the context. Let's look at those now.

Two-Feel

Playing a two-feel on a Parker blues is very easy because you'll mostly be playing nothing but root notes. There are only four measures (1, 5, 9, and 10) that contain one chord; all of the other measures contain two chords. For the latter, you just play root notes. For the former, you can play the root on beat 1 and either the 5th or perhaps the 3rd on beat 2. Here's an example of how that might sound:

EXAMPLE 1

Walking in Four

When you play with a regular walking feel, you'll have to plan ahead a bit more, but there's still not a whole lot of guesswork. For measures 1, 5, 9, and 10, standard blues walking rules apply: scale tones or arpeggios on beats 1–3 and a tone that leads to the new chord on beat 4. For all the other measures, you have only two quarter notes for each chord. That will almost always mean the root on the first beat and a tone that leads to the new chord on the second beat. Here's how that might sound.

EXAMPLE 2

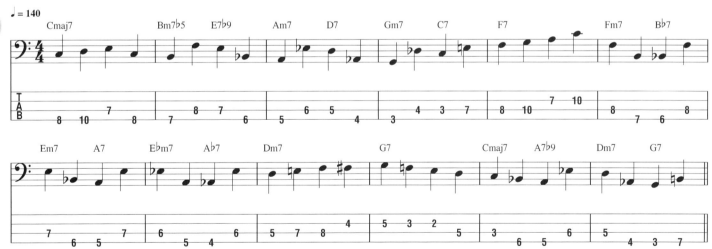

Of course, tempo is another matter. This is Charlie Parker we're talking about, so you'll need to have this down cold before you're ready to accept any challenge that comes your way! It's a refreshing set of blues changes, though, so it's worth the effort. Good luck!

LESSON #72: TEXAS BLUES

The blues of Texas is known for its big, rollicking, aggressive sound and is typified by guitar players such as Johnny Winter, Stevie Ray Vaughan, Jimmie Vaughan, Billy Gibbons, Albert Collins, and Freddie King, to name but a few. The shuffle reigns supreme, but they will mix in a good dose of slow blues and straight feels as well. Stevie Ray's "Pride and Joy" is probably the most popular example of Texas blues, but if you've been living under a rock for the past 25 years and haven't heard that tune, be sure to check out bassist Tommy Shannon's awesome playing on that song.

Equipment

With regard to bass tone, a big, round tone is most common in Texas blues. Fender Precision or Jazz basses are most common. Some players prefer flat-wound strings as well, as they will add to the darker, warmer tone. In the amp department, you'll see a bit more variation. Some prefer tube models like the Ampeg SVT or Fender Bassman, while some more modern players make use of solid-state models by Peavey, Hartke, and the like.

The Shuffle

Seeing as Texas blues is dominated by guitar players, the key of E is very common. If you can make use of the open E string in your pattern, you'll probably want to do it. Trios are common in Texas blues, and therefore the bass can usually take up more space. This often translates to playing lots of eighth notes (as opposed to mostly quarter notes) and mixing open and fretted strings.

EXAMPLE 1

Here's a typical example in E that's similar to what you'd hear Tommy Shannon play.

EXAMPLE 2

The fabulous Bill Willis, who fueled many of Freddie King's hits, including "Hideaway," had a super-cool approach that consisted of throbbing eighth notes mostly on the roots. He would occasionally decorate the line with other chord tones as well. He might come up with something like this:

Straight Feel

On a straight-eighths tune, piano-style boogie-woogie lines tend to work really well. This often includes mixing the minor and major 3rds, as well as adding the 6th.

EXAMPLE 3

Here's a typical example of this kind of thing in A. Again, eighth notes usually rule here, and the songs often don't include a turnaround, instead remaining on the I chord. There's a whole lot of position-shifting going on here, but that just adds to the excitement!

LESSON #73: CHICAGO BLUES

If you're a blues fan and haven't seen *Cadillac Records*, you need to check it out. Whether it's historically accurate is debatable, but it's still a lot of fun and is filled with great music from Chess Records artists, including Muddy Waters, Howlin' Wolf, Little Walter, Etta James, and more. Few American labels were as influential on modern blues music as Chess, with notable mentions going to Bluebird, Cobra, and Alligator.

Chicago blues are some of the leanest, meanest, and stripped-down blues of all. Generally speaking, the focus is more on the vocals and harmonica than in Texas blues, where it's typically more on the guitar. Some of the best blues vocalists of all time—Muddy Waters, Howlin' Wolf, Buddy Guy, and many more—hailed from the Chicago scene, and the music speaks for itself. If you want the hair on the back of your neck to stand on end, listen to some classic Chicago blues.

Equipment

Chicago blues dates back a ways, so many players were still playing upright bass on some of those classic recordings. The big daddy of them all is Willie Dixon, who not only played bass, but also wrote many of the hits of the day, including "Hoochie Coochie Man," "My Babe," "Spoonful," and many more.

Louis Satterfield was another session regular of the day who went on to play with many greats and eventually co-found Earth, Wind & Fire. If you're not going to haul around the upright for gigs, you'll do well with a Fender Precision or Jazz strung with flats and equipped with a foam mute. If you don't have a mute, you can just stuff a piece of foam (or just about anything similar) under your strings.

The Shuffle

As a general rule, Chicago shuffles tend to be on the quicker side, and therefore many of them are played with a two-feel or a variation thereof.

EXAMPLE 1

You'll often find a mixture of half (or quarter notes followed by a rest) and quarter notes—perhaps something like this example in the key of A:

Other Forms

Interestingly, much of the Chicago blues repertoire veers from the standard 12-bar format. Whether it's one of Muddy Waters' one-chord songs or the altered 8-bar form of Jimmy Rogers' "Walking by Myself," there's often something unique going on, which makes for some interesting riff-like lines on the bass.

EXAMPLE 2

Here's an example in G that features an unusual form that makes use of an extended I chord, followed by the V chord. This is something Muddy might have done on occasion.

Slow Blues

Few knew how to get down with the slow blues like those Chicago cats. Talk about low down! Aside from the typical, slow 12-bar blues form, they had these great, riff-driven one-chord blues that just oozed attitude and soul. While the guitar and harmonica would often play a familiar IV–♭III–I chord pattern, the bass would sometimes play a slightly different line beneath it, generating a full, rich sound.

EXAMPLE 3

You'd get things like this in the key of A:

Summary

The Chicago style ushered in the era of electric blues, and the musicians didn't hold anything back when it came to their expression. It's hard to find anyone sitting still when you break into one of those classics. You should never miss your chance to pay homage to "Sweet Home Chicago."

LESSON #74: NEW ORLEANS BLUES

As Dire Straits' Mark Knopfler eloquently stated on the band's 1991 album, *On Every Street*, everything's a bit different on the "planet of New Orleans." And music is no exception, including the blues. It just doesn't sound like anything else. It's a mixture of Caribbean rhythms, Delta blues, Dixieland, funk, and rock 'n' roll, among other things. Just like their gumbo, it's got quite a few ingredients, and it's quite spicy! Rather than guitar or harmonica, they more often feature the piano out in front, although the guitar does see action as well. Horns are often included, too. It's one big party, just like Mardi Gras!

The pianist Professor Longhair is the man to check out when you want to hear some New Orleans blues. With a career that spanned from the late '40s to his death in 1980, he did more for the New Orleans blues style than any other musician before or after him. He inspired countless New Orleans music titans, including Dr. John and Fats Domino, to name but a few.

Basic Rhythm

Much of Nawlins blues moves along at a decent clip and features highly active piano and drum parts. The bass, however, often plays it pretty simple, using mainly major triads with an added 6th tone relative to each chord. The rhythms vary slightly, but many of them are based on what's come to be known as the "rhumba blues feel," which is a straight-eighths feel that accents beat 1 and the "and" of beat 2. What comes next varies from tune to tune, but normally those accents remain.

EXAMPLE 1

Here's an example of a typical line that you might hear in the key of G:

Variations

Let's take a look at a few of the many variations that you might find. This first one is very similar to the basic form and adds the 6th at the end.

EXAMPLE 2A

EXAMPLE 2B

Here's another common way to play this riff, which involves a position shift. You can slide up to the 3rd (B) if you'd like as well.

EXAMPLE 3

Here's one that differentiates itself by accenting beats 3–4 as well. It's still built on a similar framework though.

EXAMPLE 4

Here's a modified 8-bar form that uses a feel similar to Example 3 and includes a few fills to connect some of the chords. Though many New Orleans blues don't contain a move to the V chord in the final bar, this one does—and quite a snazzy one at that!

The term jump blues refers to a blues/jazz hybrid style that peaked in the '40s with artists such as Lionel Hampton, Louis Jordan, T-Bone Walker, Big Joe Turner, and Roy Brown, to name a few. As with jazz of the day, jump blues was largely a horn-dominated music, although T-Bone was instrumental in bringing the guitar out of the rhythm section and into the spotlight. For some modern(ish), guitar-dominated examples, check out the fabulous Clarence "Gatemouth" Brown, Brian Setzer Orchestra, Hollywood Fats, and some B.B. King, among others.

Jump blues is uptempo, swingin', high-energy, and a lot of fun to play. It spun off several variants, including rock 'n' roll and rockabilly, and experienced a newfound life with the swing revival of the '90s. Obviously, you need an upright bass for the authentic jump sound, but if you must play electric, try to use flat wounds and a mute on a Fender Precision-style bass.

Form

Jump blues most often adheres to the 12-bar form, but it usually combines a bit of jazz influence with regard to the harmonic pattern. The slow change (i.e., remaining on the I chord for measures 1–4) is more common than the quick change, and the V–IV move in measures 9–10 is often replaced by a ii–V change. Since jump blues was such a horn-dominated genre, flat keys are more common than sharp keys.

Here's a typical chart in the key of B♭:

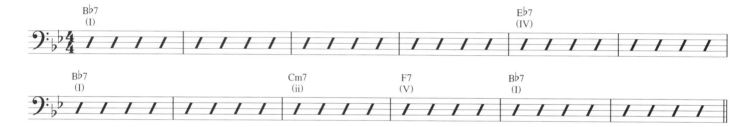

Note that many times there won't be a turnaround present or a move to the V chord in measure 12. There are exceptions to this, however.

Bass Lines

EXAMPLE 1

The most basic way to approach the jump style is to walk a boogie-style line for the majority of the chords and then switch to scalar walking for measures 9–10 to connect the ii and V chords. Here's an example of that idea. This line can be comfortably fingered in fifth position.

EXAMPLE 2

And here's a great variation to play when the form is more typical of a standard 12-bar blues. Here we have the V–IV move in measures 9–10, and the V chord shows up in measure 12 as well. Note that the only thing that's different on the I chord is that the tonic note (Bb) has been shifted up an octave, but it makes a big difference!

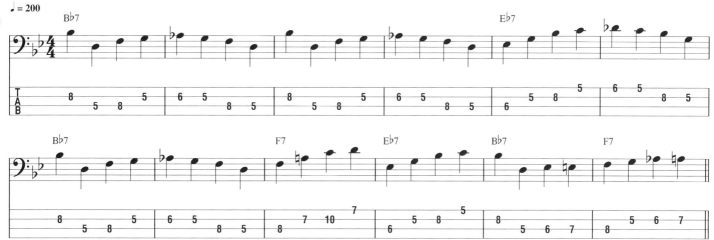

Held V Chord

Another cool variation is the held V chord, whereby measures 9–12 remain on the V and only beats 2 and 4 are struck. Here's an example of that idea, with a few other variations thrown into the earlier measures as well.

EXAMPLE 3

Summary

Jump blues is all about having fun and cuttin' loose, so try to keep that in mind when playing. To hear how this style can really cook, check out the recordings of the masters, including Louis Jordan, Lionel Hampton, Louis Prima, and Clarence "Gatemouth" Brown, among others!

LESSON #76: BLUES RIFF ROCK

The blues infused early rock heavily and continues to do so today. In the '60s, bands began using higher-wattage amps and getting louder, and the riff began to take center stage. Artists like Cream, Jimi Hendrix, the Beatles, the Rolling Stones, Led Zeppelin, and others began to mix blues forms with heavy rock riffs to create their own unique take on the genre. The guitar dominated the sound, but since the power trio was such a common format of the day (or a trio plus a singer), the bass player usually had plenty of space to fill as well.

Check out the work of Jack Bruce, Noel Redding, and John Paul Jones, among others, to hear their different approaches to this music. Some played with a pick, some with fingers, and some switched between the two, depending on the song.

Equipment

You'll generally want a bigger, rounder tone for this type of music, so vintage-style instruments tend to work best. One common model was the short-scale Gibson EB-3, which was favored heavily by Jack Bruce and also played by Bill Wyman and Andy Fraser (of Free). John Paul Jones made use of the earlier-model Gibson EB-1 (violin-shaped) as well, but did most of his work in Zeppelin with a Fender Jazz bass.

As for amplification, higher-wattage amps were generally preferred. Bruce plugged into tube-equipped Marshall 100 stacks with 4x12 cabinets, which resulted in the overdriven tone for which he would become known. John Paul Jones preferred solid-state Acoustic 360/361 amps, which were also quite loud. None of the amps were overly bright, however, and that helped achieve the warmer tones heard on those recordings.

Riffs

Much of the time, the bass and guitar played a riff in unison (or close to it) for a song's intro or verses. The riff was usually based upon the minor pentatonic or blues scale. In this lesson, we'll work out of A, but these riffs can be transposed to any key. Here are a few commonly used fingerings for A minor pentatonic:

A Minor Pentatonic

Bands often would take a riff and apply it to the 12-bar bar blues form, basically transposing it to fit each chord and making minor adjustments if needed.

EXAMPLE 1

For example, you might get something like this:

EXAMPLE 2

Sometimes the guitar and bass will play in unison for one measure and then break into separate parts for the next. Something like this:

EXAMPLE 3

Another cool idea is a riff in which only the low root note changes—the rest of it is repeated nearly verbatim throughout. This can sound great as an interlude. Here's an example of that idea:

LESSON #77: ENSEMBLE HITS

In jazzier blues styles, such as jump or rockabilly, it's very common for the band to engage in a series of ensemble hits. These rhythmic exclamations, usually punctuated with horn blasts, can occur during intros, verses, or behind a solo, so you've got to be prepared. You'll hear this type of stuff all over recordings of the '40s and '50s, and it can really kick a tune into high gear.

You'll almost always have a chart or be expected to know the song if it's going to contain this type of thing, but in the rare event that you don't, there are some cues that you can keep an eye out for:

1. **Watch the horn players:** If they all step up to the mic at the end of a chorus and get ready to play, chances are there might be an ensemble section approaching.

2. **Watch the drummer:** He may be looking around to signal a rhythmic figure coming up.

3. **Stay alert:** If you miss the beginning of a rhythmic hit, don't panic. Chances are, it will be repeated the same way throughout the chorus, so if you're listening carefully, you can join in perfectly the second time.

Conventions

Although these ensemble figures are often composed specifically for each song, there are certain conventions—just like the 12-bar blues form itself—that are often followed.

1. They're usually brief, lasting only a few beats each time.

2. They usually appear at consistent intervals with regard to measure numbers. There are two common structures in this regard: measures 1, 3, 5, 7, 9, and 11 (every other measure), and measures 1, 5, and 9 (every four measures).

3. *Everyone* joins in on the hits—even the bass player.

The Bassist's Role

Unless there's a specific chart indicating a precise part for you to play, it normally sounds great to simply hit the root of the chord in the specified rhythm and then resume your standard line until the next hit. Let's look at a few examples of this in the key of C.

Here's a typical chart indicating this type of thing:

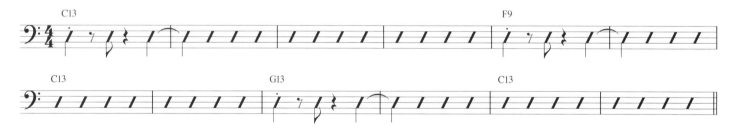

Now let's take a look at what you might play if you were reading this chart.

EXAMPLE 1

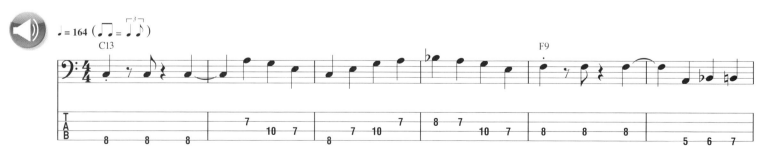

The hardest part is keeping track of your normal walking pattern and resuming it in a natural way—you want to be sure that you're back to hitting the root on the right beat, etc. This will take a bit of practice. To get used to this idea, try laying out for different intervals (i.e., beats) and then resuming the walking pattern. The laying out will substitute for the ensemble hits.

For example, lay out for measure 1 and then resume on the downbeat of measure 2. Then, lay out for measure 5 and resume on the downbeat of measure 6, etc. Or you may have a rhythmic figure that only lasts two or three beats. So lay out for beats 1–3 of measure 1 and resume on beat 4. Do the same for measures 5 and 9, etc.

Once you get familiar with resuming the walk on different beats, you can simply plug in the ensemble hits where you were normally laying out.

When the figures appear every other measure, it's a little easier to connect the chords because you don't really need to resume a walking pattern—you can simply use the remaining part of the measure to lead into the next chord. Here's an example of that idea:

EXAMPLE 2

So any time we weren't playing the hits, we were simply ascending chromatically into the approaching chord. You can play around with variations on this same idea.

Summary

These ensemble figures are a blast to play when everyone is in sync. It's a really big, full sound, and it can lift a song to a whole other level. Again, check out the jazz-blues recordings of the '40s and '50s to hear these in action. And, if you're subbing on a gig and they call an old jump blues with which you're not familiar, you might want to quickly ask the drummer if there are any rhythmic hits that you'll need to know about. Stay alert, and you'll catch on quickly!

LESSON #78: PLAYING IN A TRIO

For blues music, the trio has become a classic group format, with drums, bass, and guitar by far the most common combination in modern times. The trio has several advantages with regard to the blues:

▶ **It's agile:** With so few players, it's much easier to improvise as a unit, which is a huge part of the blues vocabulary.

▶ **It's portable:** All you need is a small stage in the corner of a smoky bar, and you're good to go!

▶ **It allows for maximum expression on all levels:** With such lean instrumentation, each member is really afforded the room to stretch out and fill up as much sonic space as they'd like.

In this lesson, we'll take a look at some of the aspects involved in playing bass with a trio: the freedoms, the dangers, the good, the bad, and the ugly.

Perhaps the most important thing you'll notice when initially playing with a trio is how much room there is to wiggle. The fewer instruments you have, the more this is true. If you're playing with just a guitarist and drummer, chances are you're never going to be stepping on the toes of either one—unless, of course, you decide for some reason to break into a solo in 19th position while the guitarist is trying to sing. In that case, you might want to start looking for a new gig!

When the guitarist is soloing, you're the sole provider of the harmony. This means a few things:

▶ You really don't want to screw up because it's going to be very noticeable!

▶ You need to nail the roots at the right spot so that there's little doubt of where you are in the form.

▶ Try to keep your fills fairly chord-based so that the harmony is still implied.

Shuffles

So let's say you're backing a guitar solo on a moderate shuffle blues in A. If you've stuck to the fairly traditional boogie lines throughout the verses, you can feel free to step out a bit and get a little more colorful behind the solo if you'd like, but you've got to keep things on a fairly short leash because you don't want to leave any doubt as to what the harmony is at a given time. A simple rule of thumb is: you either need to be establishing a chord or leading to another one. You don't want to be caught in between those two concepts because that's where you can get into trouble.

EXAMPLE 1

Here's an example that demonstrates how you may take a bit of liberty with the bass line while still remaining firmly entrenched in the harmony at hand.

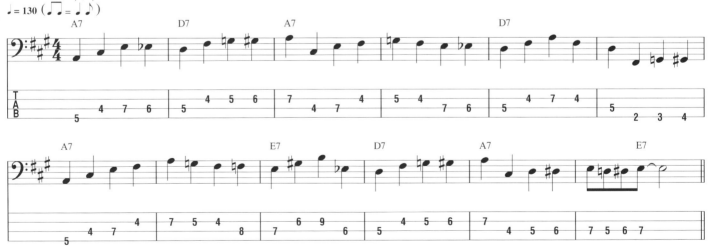

Look over that line closely. Every note is either establishing a harmony (i.e., it's a chord tone) or it's part of a line that's obviously leading somewhere. The good news is that the blues is so firmly entrenched in us that usually everyone knows what's supposed to come next. So as long as you're heading somewhere, people are usually glad to go along for the ride. However, that also means that it's very easy for the audience to recognize when you screw up something important—like the wrong note on the downbeat!

Funky Blues

Funky blues is particularly fun in a trio format because you can really stretch out and play some interesting things, so long as you hit the important signposts along the way. One common method is to play the established groove (from the verse, for example) but embellish it with fills along the way.

EXAMPLE 2

Here's an example of that idea in C. Measure 1 presents the basic groove intact, but we take some liberties throughout by decorating it will fills that lead somewhere. The turnaround is especially fun and funky.

Slow Blues

The slow blues is kind of the proving ground for a soloist, so it's really important that we provide a firm foundation upon which they can build their improvisations. This doesn't mean that we don't have the freedom to roam around a bit here and there, because we do, but it's just that much more critical that we provide clear, unambiguous harmony when it counts.

Summary

To summarize, here are things to keep in mind when playing in a trio:

▶ You can fill more space than usual with regard to tone, notes, register, and rhythms because of the limited instrumentation.

▶ Mistakes on your part are amplified, so you have to be on your game!

▶ When you're playing behind a solo, you're the sole harmony provider, so do the soloist proud!

If you keep these things in mind, you should have a lot of fun playing in this format. It really is something unique when you find three players that gel especially well. Good luck!

VARIETY IS THE SPICE OF BLUES

With anything we do in life, it's important to maintain a fresh perspective so we don't end up feeling bored or in a rut. Music is no different, and this is perhaps especially true with the blues due to its fairly limited format and harmonic structure. Therefore, it's nice to think of ways that you can challenge yourself while still serving the greater good of the song. In this lesson, we'll look at several ideas that you can implement in this regard.

Fretboard Positions

The first concept is perhaps the most obvious, but it's often overlooked because of a little thing called habit. How many times have you played a slow blues or a shuffle in G? Do you tend to start it off the same way each time? Why not play it a different way to see what happens? For example, take this line:

EXAMPLE 1A

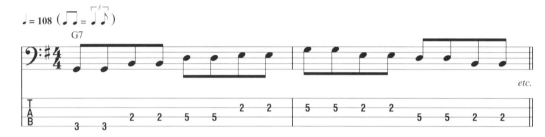

Sure, it's very efficient to play it that way since it sits nicely in second position. But, if you try it another way, you'll end up in a different part of the neck. Besides the slightly different sound you'd achieve, it could open the doors to other ideas like different bass lines or even a variation on your tried-and-true one.

EXAMPLE 1B

You could play everything in Example 1B in second position, of course, but you may not think to do it if you're avoiding old habits.

Play Fewer Notes

This is especially applicable to funky blues, where we can tend to get a bit note-y. It may seem counter-intuitive, but the fewer notes you play, the more time you have to think. When we play a super busy bass line, we're normally just stringing together lines or ideas that we already know. But when we put restrictions on ourselves, by limiting the notes that we can play on each chord, for example, we're forced to think about how they're really going to affect the groove.

As a nice exercise, try limiting yourself to, say, three notes per measure (not counting dead notes). You could play them in any rhythm that you want, but you only get three per measure. You might be surprised by how much it can still groove!

EXAMPLE 2

The idea is to separate the essential from the fluff. If you get a bass solo during the night, that's your chance to strut your stuff. Otherwise, your primary objective is to groove—not to show off. So strip it down and start simple. Then complicate it where it needs it—not the other way around.

Ornaments

Oftentimes a simple grace note can spice up an otherwise stock phrase. This isn't something you'd want to do all the time, but it can provide a nice bit of ear candy at certain times, and that's often just what the doctor ordered. To hear this, compare measures A and B:

EXAMPLE 3

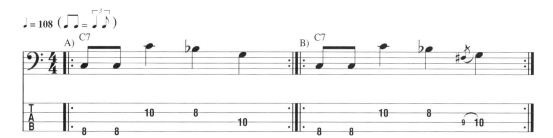

Summary

Blues may be repetitive at times, but that doesn't mean you always have to repeat yourself. If you make a conscious effort to keep it fresh, you'll never get bored—and you may even end up developing your own recognizable style in the process. Have fun and experiment!

Blues music is largely about subtlety, and therefore it's nice to be able to use as many tools as possible to make the music come alive. You can do plenty with note choices and rhythms for sure, but dynamics can play a huge role as well. In this lesson, we'll talk about what I call pluck-hand dynamics, which is a catch-all term for volume and tonal fluctuations achievable with the plucking hand. You've got a lot of versatility in the plucking hand, so it's time to unleash it!

Moving Along the String

By simply moving your plucking finger forward (toward the neck) or back (toward the bridge), you can achieve quite a variety of tones. Depending on the context (lowdown blues vs. modern slick blues, etc.), one extreme will probably sound better than the other. And then there are, of course, many shades of gray in between for fine-tuning the sound.

EXAMPLE 1

Let's take a listen to the same line, first plucked near the bridge (see photo A) and then near the neck (see photo B).

Plucking near the bridge

Plucking near the neck

These two extremes demonstrate the range that's available to us at any time. Yet many players plant their hand in the same spot and never think twice about it. If you need your line to sound a bit more aggressive, try moving toward the bridge and digging in a bit more. If you want a rounder, fatter tone, try moving toward the neck a bit. You'll find that, along with the combinations of pickups (if your bass is equipped with more than one) and volume/tone controls, you've got a huge assortment of tones at your fingertips.

Plucking with the Thumb While Palm Muting

Another great sound, especially when the dynamics have come way down in a song, is plucking with the thumb while palm muting. To use this technique, rest your plucking-hand palm on the string where it contacts the bridge. The farther you move in from the bridge, the more muted the sound will be. Experiment with different positions until you find the sound you want.

Pluck the strings with your thumb, using a downward motion

EXAMPLE 2

Check out the difference in sound. First, you'll hear this line played normally, and then you'll hear it with the palm mute.

Summary

It's easy to forget about subtle touches like this and just get on auto-pilot with the plucking hand. But when applied, these subtleties really do add another dimension to the sound. It's not going to knock you over the head or anything, but then again, neither does changing amps or basses, and players do that all the time. If you get into the habit of listening for and creating the subtleties in music, your overall musical experience will grow by leaps and bounds.

LESSON #81: EQUIPMENT PRIMER

If you're new to blues bass guitar, you may be wondering what comprises the best-sounding rig. While this is always a very personal and subjective topic, there are certainly instruments and amps that have proven themselves in the genre time and again. In this lesson, we'll dissect the common blues bass rig and examine its innards to see what makes it tick (or thump).

The Bass

Let's start with the obvious. You can't call yourself a bass guitarist without a bass!

UPRIGHT

During the early years—roughly before the mid-'50s—the upright, or double bass, reigned supreme in the blues. You can hear this sound all over the early recordings of Muddy Waters, Howlin' Wolf, Willie Dixon, Lionel Hampton, etc. Plywood models, such as the King Moretone (Dixon's bass of choice) with gut strings, were common.

Although the electric bass has greatly surpassed the upright in the music world, there are still plenty of upright players around, particularly in blues, since it's such a close relative of jazz, which still employs the upright a great deal. You'll also find them in rockabilly groups, such as the Brian Setzer Orchestra (Johnny Hatton) or the Reverend Horton Heat (Jimbo Wallace).

ELECTRIC

Although the modern electric bass had been around since the late '30s, it didn't take off until Fender introduced the Precision bass in 1951. By the mid-'50s, after witnessing the success of Fender's "P-bass," Gibson had introduced their own electric bass, which was violin shaped (a precursor to the Höfner 500/1 "Beatle Bass" made famous by Paul McCartney) and featured painted F-holes to make it resemble a miniature version of the double bass.

The Fender Precision (P-bass) reigned supreme throughout the '50s and most of the '60s in the blues world (and many other styles as well!), so you simply can't go wrong with a P-bass or something similar. Although some players do make use of the Fender Jazz Bass (introduced in 1960), they're not nearly as common as the P-bass. If you'd like a more authentic tone, you should string it with flat-wounds, as they were all that was widely available back then. In fact, many players still prefer them today due to their tone and feel—and the fact that they can last years.

Fender Precision Bass

Amps

The only amps available when the electric bass arrived were tube amps, so it makes sense that, if you want the authentic tone found on those old recordings, you should use a tube amp. Back in the day, by far the most widely recorded bass amp of all was the Ampeg B-15 Portaflex (and its various models), introduced in 1960. This amp had a unique design in which the electronics were mounted inside the speaker cabinet, hanging from the top. When you were ready to play, you could open the cabinet and flip the top panel over, revealing the amp "head."

Another common amp choice of the day was the Fender Bassman. You don't see as many of those in bassists' rigs today, but they've become extremely sought-after as a guitar amp!

Ampeg B-15

Fender Bassman

Just about any vintage-style tube amp will get you close enough, so don't feel the need to break the bank on a prized vintage amp—unless you really want to! Many players have made effective use of solid-state amps (e.g., Hartke, Gallien-Krueger, Acoustic) since then, so don't feel left out if you can't afford/don't prefer a tube amp. While we can be informed by the choices made by those who came before us, when it comes down to it, you should use whatever you feel helps achieve the sound you want.

Summary

The saying often goes that "tone is in the hands," and this is certainly true to some extent. But in order to recreate the sounds that we've heard on countless recordings, it only makes sense to use the tools that they used to achieve them. That said, the tools won't learn to play for you; you've got to handle that yourself! Good luck and have fun on your tone quest.

LESSON #82: BASS LINE STRATEGIES FOR THE I CHORD

Each measure in the 12-bar blues form has some purpose, and it's important to know what that is when creating our bass lines. The more aware we are, the better prepared we'll be in terms of the effectiveness of our lines. In this lesson, we'll look at the I chord specifically. It shows up several times in the typical 12-bar form, and each time its function changes slightly. Although we're working with a shuffle here, the basic concepts should be transferable to slow blues, funk blues, etc. We'll work in the key of G for the sake of simplicity and use quarter notes, but you can add eighth notes as you see fit. All of the measures are numbered in the examples for clarity.

Before we get started, let's look at the most common variations on the 12-bar form so we can identify when and where the I chord may show up.

STANDARD 12-BAR BLUES

I	I	I	I
IV	IV	I	I
V	IV	I	V

QUICK CHANGE

I	IV	I	I
IV	IV	I	I
V	IV	I	V

NO TURNAROUND

I	I	I	I
IV	IV	I	I
V	IV	I	I

There are other variations, such as the extended V chord, whereby measure 10 remains on the V chord instead of moving to the IV, but they don't affect the I chord, so we'll leave them out for now.

Measures 1–4

Depending on whether it's a standard 12-bar blues or a quick change, we'll sometimes treat the I chord in measure 1 differently, so let's look at both. In a standard 12-bar blues, you have four full measures of the I chord up front, which is quite a bit of time. The first three measures will establish the I-chord harmony (in our case, G7), while measure 4 should lead us to the IV chord, C7. The standard boogie patterns happen to do both of these well.

EXAMPLE 1A

EXAMPLE 1B

EXAMPLE 2

In regard to measure 4, where we need to lead to the IV (C7) chord, we have lots of other options available as well. Here are just a few:

With a quick change, the first measure not only establishes the tonic chord, it also leads to the IV chord. So, aside from all the standard boogie patterns, which will work fine, you could also use any of the ideas from Example 2 if you wanted a slightly jazzier sound.

Measures 7–8

For measures 7–8, you could play a standard two-bar boogie pattern if you'd like. But if you want measure 8 to *really* lead into the V chord, you can employ some other ideas. Here are several options for measures 7–8:

EXAMPLE 3

Measures 11–12

If a turnaround is present, you generally have two basic options available for measure 11: ascending (A) or descending (B).

EXAMPLE 4

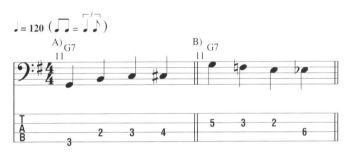

If no turnaround is present, you have several options. You could play a standard two-bar boogie phrase, and it will sound fine. This is especially common for faster tempos. But you could also treat it as a two-bar excursion from—and back to—the I chord.

EXAMPLE 5

Here are some examples that demonstrate that idea. You generally want to try to hit a chord tone on the downbeat of both measures, but beyond that, you can take some liberty.

Summary

So basically, you have a whole lot of options available for the I chord. While the tried-and-true patterns certainly work fine, it's nice to be able to spice things up when you want. Try mixing and matching these ideas in different combinations to see what sounds good to you.

LESSON #83: BASS LINE STRATEGIES FOR THE IV CHORD

In this lesson, we're going to take a look at some different ideas for creating bass lines over the IV chord. We'll work in the key of G for simplicity's sake (so the IV chord will be C), and although we'll be using a moderate shuffle groove here, you can adapt these concepts to most other blues styles as well. These lines will consist of nothing but quarter notes, but feel free to add eighth notes as you see fit. All of the measures are numbered in the examples for clarity.

Before we get started, let's look at the most common variations on the 12-bar blues form so we can identify when and where the IV chord may show up. We'll only look at the variations in which the IV chord's presence is affected.

STANDARD 12-BAR BLUES

I	I	I	I
IV	IV	I	I
V	IV	I	V

QUICK CHANGE

I	IV	I	I
IV	IV	I	I
V	IV	I	V

NO TURNAROUND

I	I	I	I
IV	IV	I	I
V	IV	I	I

QUICK CHANGE WITH NO TURNAROUND

I	IV	I	I
IV	IV	I	I
V	IV	I	I

EXTENDED V CHORD

I	I	I	I
IV	IV	I	I
V	V	I	V

QUICK CHANGE WITH EXTENDED V CHORD

I	IV	I	I
IV	IV	I	I
V	V	I	V

There are two measures in which the IV chord always shows up (measures 5–6) and two places where it sometimes shows up (measure 2 and measure 10).

Measure 2

In a quick-change blues, we head right to the IV chord at measure 2. This chord not only establishes the IV-chord harmony, it can also lead back to the I chord. The most basic idea is to simply transpose the boogie line from the I chord to the IV chord, like this:

EXAMPLE 1

While this works fine with respect to establishing the IV chord, it doesn't do much to acknowledge the approaching I chord in measure 3. The one exception to this is if you begin measure 3 with the G note in the higher octave. In this case, the A note on beat 4 of measure 2 leads nicely to it.

EXAMPLE 2

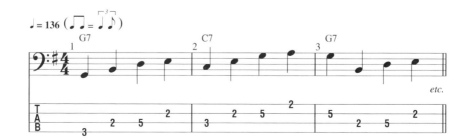

What other ways can we think of for leading back to the I chord? Here are some possibilities:

EXAMPLE 3

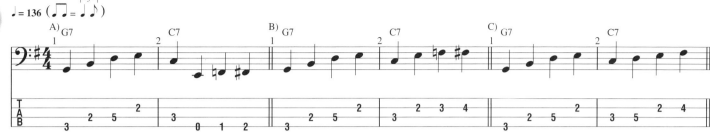

Measures 5–6

At this point, the harmony has fully shifted to the IV chord—for the longest stretch in the whole 12-bar blues—so firmly establishing the chord here with a two-bar phrase works well. The typical boogie patterns work great in that respect.

EXAMPLE 4

Another option is to establish the IV-chord harmony in measure 5 and then use measure 6 to lead back to the I chord. This is a jazzier approach. You'll get something like these ideas:

EXAMPLE 5

Measure 10

If the IV chord appears in measure 10, it's usually functioning as a passing harmony between the V and I chords, and therefore it can work well on its own or by leading to the I chord. Any of the transposable boogie patterns will work, such as those in measure 5 of Example 4's figures, or you could make use of the phrases that lead back to the I chord, as found in measure 2 of Example 3's figures.

Summary

It's nice to have options available when creating bass lines for a blues tune. The more you have in your trick bag, the freer you'll be to improvise when you're on stage and the tempos are creeping up. Try combining these ideas to see what you can come up with. Enjoy!

BASS LINE STRATEGIES FOR THE V CHORD

In this lesson, we'll take a look at some ideas for generating bass lines on the V chord. Some of these may be old hat, but others may be entirely new or at least different enough to spark some other ideas of your own. We'll work in the key of G for simplicity's sake (so the V chord will be D), and although we'll be using a moderate shuffle groove here, you can adapt these concepts to most other blues styles as well. These lines will consist of nothing but quarter notes, but feel free to add eighth notes as you see fit. All of the measures are numbered in the examples for clarity.

Before we get started, let's look at the most common variations on the 12-bar blues form so we can identify when and where the V chord may show up.

STANDARD 12-BAR BLUES			
I	I	I	I
IV	IV	I	I
V	IV	I	V

NO TURNAROUND			
I	I	I	I
IV	IV	I	I
V	IV	I	I

EXTENDED V CHORD			
I	I	I	I
IV	IV	I	I
V	V	I	V

Of course, all of these variations come in the quick-change variety (with the IV chord in measure 2) as well, but we haven't listed them because they don't affect the V chord.

To recap: the V chord is present in measure 9, sometimes in measure 10, and sometimes in measure 12.

Measures 9–10

Measure 9 marks the first instance of the V chord in the standard 12-bar blues form, so it's important to establish its tonality strongly. All of the standard boogie lines do this well.

EXAMPLE 1

Example C also leads nicely to the IV chord via a half step. If you'd like to lead to the IV chord smoothly, there are other options as well, such as these:

EXAMPLE 2

The last one (example D) works particularly well if, on beat 2 of measure 10, you walk up from the open E to G.

If you have an extended V chord for measures 9–10, then you have a bit more time to establish the V harmony. Standard two-bar boogie lines will often lead nicely to the I chord of measure 11 on their own.

EXAMPLE 3

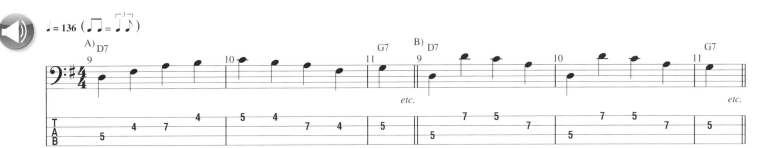

If you want to use measure 10 to lead back to the I chord, you have several other options available. Here are just a few ideas:

EXAMPLE 4

Measure 12

If there's a turnaround, the V chord will usually appear on the "and" of beat 2, but it will occasionally appear on the downbeat of beats 1 or 2. If it's a standard turnaround, beat 1 will have the V chord in the bass, but the actual chord will be the I chord. In our case, this would be G/D (or G7/D). The actual V chord is reached on the "and" of beat 2, usually via chromatic motion (see example A). When the actual V chord hits on the downbeat, you can walk up or down to the I chord (see examples B and C). When it hits on beat 2, there's usually a specified phrase worked out in place of a traditional turnaround in measure 11 and you'll sustain a half note on beat 2 of measure 12 before adding one more D note on beat 4 (see example D).

EXAMPLE 5

LESSON #85: ADDING THE 6TH

The 6th is a colorful and useful note that we can use in our bass-line patterns. It not only provides a different flavor than the basic major triad or dominant seventh arpeggios, it's also very functional as a passing tone in certain applications when we need to get from one place to another. In this lesson, we'll examine the note in several contexts and learn to make the most effective use of it.

The Basic Boogie

The most basic boogie pattern that we can play would contain only the notes of the major triad: the root, 3rd, and 5th. In the case of a C chord, this would be C (root), E (3rd), and G (5th).

EXAMPLE 1

When we play this type of line, it's very lean and simple-sounding.

EXAMPLE 2

By adding the 6th (A) on beat 4, instead of going back down to the 3rd, we liven up the line quite a bit.

Variations

If we extend our thinking a bit, we see that we have four different notes: C, E, G, and A. So, if we walk up four notes and come down four, we'll end up with a nice two-bar phrase.

EXAMPLE 3

With just this much material—the four different notes and the octave C—we can generate many variations by mixing things up a bit. Here are just a few two-bar ideas:

EXAMPLE 4

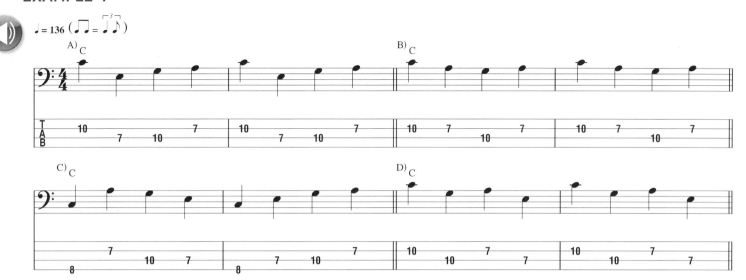

This is just the tip of the iceberg. You can come up with many more ideas by just being creative. By combining the standard triad with the sixth chord, we can create some great four-bar phrases that really take the listener somewhere.

EXAMPLE 5

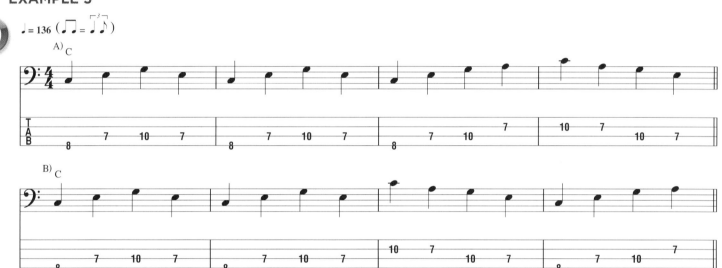

Using the Low 6th on the IV and V Chords

If you're playing a blues in C out of seventh position, as we've been doing, you can get a great sound by reaching down below the IV and V chords instead of always playing above them. Our final example demonstrates this kind of idea.

EXAMPLE 6

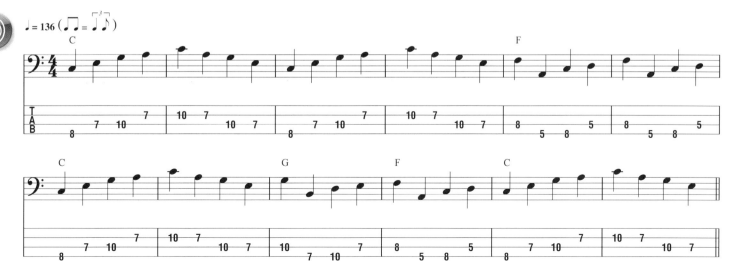

ADDING THE 9TH

There are a number of ways we can dress up the typical boogie bass patterns. One way is by using colorful notes. The 9th is particularly interesting in this regard. Though it needs to be handled with care and, in some cases, used sparingly, it can really take a line to another level. In this lesson, we'll examine how to get the most out of this special note. We'll work in the key of C for the sake of simplicity, but you can transpose these lines to any key.

Theory Review

What do we mean by the 9th? It's an interval that refers to the musical distance between notes. The interval of a 9th means that it spans nine note names. If we look at the C major scale and count nine notes, starting from the root, we'll end up with D.

You may have also noticed that D was the second note as well. This is true. The reason we're calling D the "9th" is because we're going to be playing it in the next octave; that is, we're going to be playing lines in which we'll span more than an octave on one chord. There's a little more to it than that, but that explanation will suffice for our needs.

Tips and Guidelines

We don't want to just play the 9th whenever it strikes our fancy. If we're not careful, we can obscure the harmony and confuse the listener. In other words, it can sound like a mistake if not done right. Here are some tips to help you out in this regard:

▶ You generally don't want to hang on the 9th for more than a quarter note, depending on the tempo. The faster the tempo, the more you can get away with, note-wise.

▶ You usually want to follow the 9th with a strong chord tone in order to resolve the tension that you've created.

▶ It can lose its effectiveness if repeated often; therefore, it's best to use it sparingly.

Funk-Blues Grooves

In general, the 9th is better suited to funkier grooves because the dominant ninth chord (often played by guitarists and/or keyboardists) is a common sound. It's also generally more active, rhythmically speaking, so we can sneak some things in while remaining fairly inconspicuous. Let's take a look at a few examples that make use of the 9th.

EXAMPLE 1

This first example uses the 9th for the I (C9) chord and transposes the same idea for the IV (F9) chord, for which the 9th is the note G.

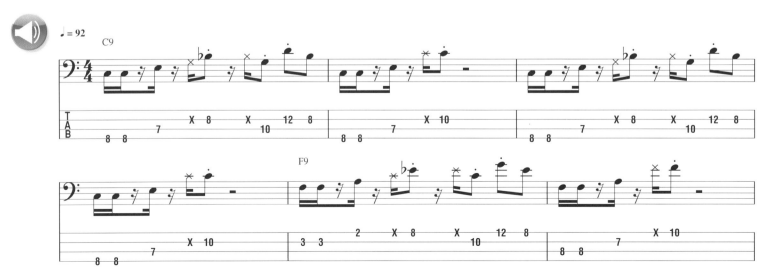

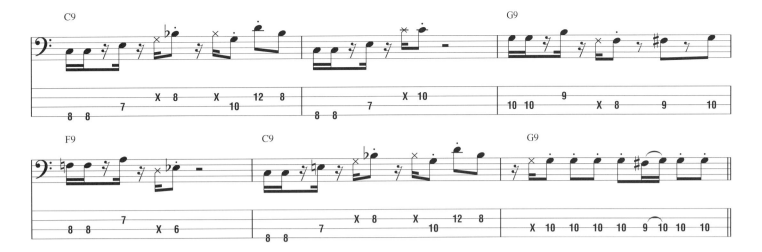

EXAMPLE 2

This example is sparser, but the 9th still colors the line heavily.

Shuffle Grooves

The 9th can be incorporated into the shuffle as well, but you have to be careful so that you're not obscuring the harmony too much. The faster the tempo, the more liberty you can take in this regard.

EXAMPLE 3

In this example, the 9th is featured only once (measure 4), but it makes quite a statement.

VARIATIONS ON THE 12-BAR FORM

Though the tried-and-true 12-bar form remains in wide use and shows no sign of letting up, you'll occasionally run across variations on this form that merit investigation. We'll call the standard form one in which you have the typical I, IV, and V chords. In this lesson, we'll take a look at some common (and maybe not so common) variations on this form and learn how to best handle them from the low-end perspective. We'll work in the key of E for this lesson, but these ideas are transposable to any key. Also, we won't include variations on the turnaround in this lesson, as that topic can fill another lesson entirely.

IV-Chord Inversion in Measure 10

This doesn't change the actual harmony, but it changes what we play, and it's a very cool sound. You'll find this one most often in a slow blues. The idea is that, instead of descending from the root of the V chord in measure 9 to the root of the IV chord in measure 10, we move up a step to the 3rd of the IV chord in measure 10. This places the chord in first inversion (3rd on bottom) and makes it sound big and fat.

EXAMPLE 1

In this example, we'll pick it up in measure 7 of the form, which means we'll have two measures of the I chord before going to the V.

ii–V in Measures 9–10

This one is common in jump blues and more uptown-sounding blues. Instead of playing the V–IV change in measures 9–10, you play ii–V. In the key of E, this translates to F#m7–B7. The most common bass line, which is almost always played for this variation, walks up from the root of the ii chord to the root of the V chord by way of a chromatic passing tone and then walks down the scale from the V to the I.

EXAMPLE 2

You'll also occasionally see this variation with a dominant II chord (F#7). In this case, you can substitute the following line for measure 9. The descending line in measure 10 would be the same.

♭VII in Measure 2 and II–IV in Measures 9–10

This is a unique one that sounds very interesting. You may find one of these variations without the other, but they seem to appear most often as a set, so I've included them together. The line for the I chord is normally transposed verbatim down a whole step for the ♭VII chord. In measure 9, a major triad (1–3–5) or dominant seventh arpeggio (1–3–5–♭7) is often played for the II chord, and a walking line handles the IV chord similar to the way it would in measure 2 or 6.

EXAMPLE 3

Summary

Though this really is only the tip of the iceberg, it gives you a good idea of the many variations that can exist within the 12-bar format. As long as certain checkpoints are hit along the way—the I chord in measure 1, the IV chord in measure 5, and the I chord again in measure 7—it's most likely going to sound like a 12-bar blues. That said, nearly endless variations can occur elsewhere.

VARIATIONS ON THE TURNAROUND

Just like the 12-bar blues itself, the turnaround is the subject of countless variations. And it always helps to be familiar with as many of them as you can because you never know when one of them will show up in a tune. If you want to be hired back, you'd better be able to recognize it immediately and hop onboard!

In this lesson, we'll take a look at some ways the turnaround can be chewed up, turned around, and spit out. We'll work in the key of A.

The Basics

The function of the turnaround is to "turn the progression around" back to the beginning again. As such, the basic movement is the I chord in measure 11 moving to the V chord in measure 12. The two obvious variations are the ascending version and the descending version. The bass plays either 1–3–4–♯4–5 or 1–♭7–6–♭6–5.

ASCENDING

DESCENDING

Variation 1: I–IV–I–V

This is most common turnaround variation in a slow blues. Instead of the walk-up or walk-down in measure 11, we have the I chord for two beats and the IV chord for two beats. The I chord shows up again on beat 1 of measure 12, followed on beat 3 by the V chord.

EXAMPLE 1

Variation 2: I–VI–ii–V

This is the turnaround from a jazz-blues, but you'll sometimes find this thrown into an otherwise standard I–IV–V 12-bar blues. When it shows up, you can just walk through it with roots and leading tones.

EXAMPLE 2

Variation 3: I–♭III–II–♭II

This is another jazzy one, but guitarists are more likely to play this because it just involves moving the same chord around chromatically. And you can follow suit by just pounding out the root notes.

EXAMPLE 3A

You'll occasionally hear this one as a double-time variation. In other words, this chromatic line will replace the normal ascending or descending line in measure 11.

EXAMPLE 3B

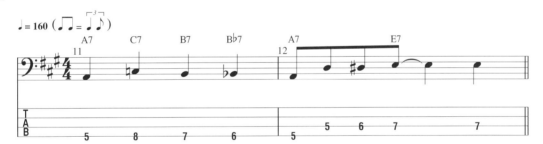

Variation 4: I–♭iii°–ii–V

This is another jazzy one, but it sounds really great and does show up occasionally in more standard-ish blues.

EXAMPLE 4

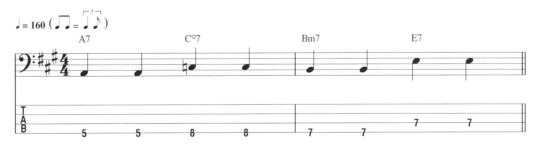

Summary

The bottom line: you can *never* know too many turnarounds! It's the one spot of the 12-bar blues where things tend to get fancy—if they're going to at all. So after you've learned these, keep on the lookout for any others that strike your fancy. Learn them and try them out on your next jam session. Impress your friends!

LESSON #89: DOUBLE STOPS

When playing in a blues trio and the guitarist takes off on a solo, there's nothing else providing the harmony but you. While the wide-open sound of bass and lead guitar has its own charm and has been heard on countless stages and recordings over the years, it's also fun to provide a bit more in the way of accompaniment at times. In this lesson, we'll look at how you can do just that with double stops. The double-stop shapes that we'll mostly be using here are the tritone, the perfect 5th, and the major 6th. We'll mostly be using the higher strings in an upper register to avoid the sound becoming too muddy.

Tritone

Here are several tritones, each on different string sets.

Perfect 5th and Major 6th

We'll be using these two intervals together. Here's what they look like:

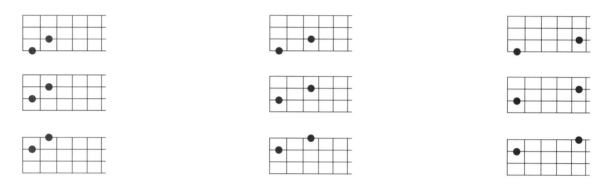

Here are three double-stop examples. You can pluck them with an upstroke of the finger, a downstroke with the thumb, or with a plectrum if you'd like.

EXAMPLE 1

EXAMPLE 2

♩ = 61

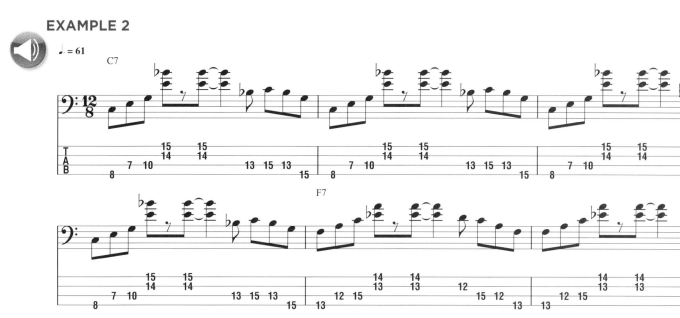

EXAMPLE 3

♩ = 92

LESSON #90: LISTEN TO THE SOLOIST

Along with jazz, the blues is one of the most improvisational musical styles around. Therefore, it makes sense that the best bands are ones that are in sync with each other, helping each other sound better by accenting strengths, covering deficiencies, supporting ideas, and so on. If you took a famous guitar or harmonica solo and put it over a different backing band, the result would be quite different. The rhythm section is a huge part of why the solo cooks or doesn't cook. In this lesson, we'll look at how we can help the soloist sound his or her best during their moment in the spotlight.

First: What Not to Do

Here's an example of a guitar soloist who clearly yearns for some dynamic interaction from his rhythm section, but they've all but fallen asleep. They're not responding at all to his changes in volume or energy, and the result is an empty shell of what it could be.

SLEEPING RHYTHM SECTION

Now let's have a listen to the same exact guitar solo but played with a rhythm section that's paying attention and responding to what they're hearing. The difference is pretty much night and day.

RESPONSIVE RHYTHM SECTION

So what changed? Simply put, the bassist and drummer were listening and interacting. While there are times when your job is to be nothing but a steady rock, playing the same thing over and over, a searing blues solo is usually not one of those times. It's your chance to become one with the soloist and work *with* him or her in creating a memorable musical statement.

A Few Tips and Strategies

Let's take a look at some specific tips that will help us engage a bit more.

Volume

The first and most obvious tip deals with volume. It sounds simple, but some players just tend to switch on auto pilot and forget to listen and react. If the soloist is playing softly, he wants you to play softly. If he really starts digging in, it means he wants more volume from everyone—not just his guitar.

EXAMPLE 1

Don't Compete

Sometimes when the soloist is really cutting loose and obviously building up to a climax, it's best to play something fairly simple—even repeating the same note—to help stay out of the way and keep the focus on what he's building. If all of a sudden you decide to pull out your fanciest tapping lick, it could be a bit distracting, to say the least.

EXAMPLE 2

Reinforce When You Can

If you hear the soloist repeating an obvious rhythm, jump in on it with the drummer if you can. It will make the idea sound huge instantly! This can be as simple as hitting one specific beat each measure or as complex as following the soloist on a repetitive, syncopated rhythm that takes three or four measures to turn around.

EXAMPLE 3

Here's a relatively simple example in which the bass and drums lock onto an upbeat rhythm played by the soloist.

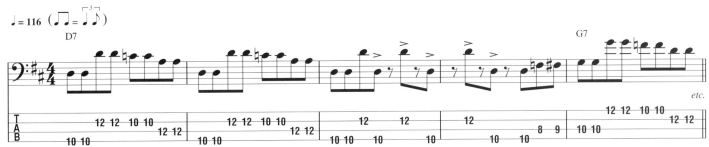

EXAMPLE 4

Here's an example that's a bit more advanced. This type of thing usually takes either some very experienced players or a band that's been playing together for a while. You need to be able to keep your place in the measure and make sure you come out at the right time. If the drummer joins in on the rhythm, as is the case here, there'll be nothing to indicate where beat 1 is anymore!

Summary

Playing together is much more fun when the band is in sync. And the only way to get there is to listen closely and interact with each other. Don't phone it in! It's much more rewarding to be creative with the soloist instead of being his karaoke jam track. Some other ideas include echoing his licks—if he's leaving a lot of space—or cutting heads! Of course, you'll likely need to feel this out before you'd try it onstage, but the point is that the possibilities for interaction are many. Enjoy!

LESSON #91: THINKING AHEAD

Although the blues seems like fairly basic music—usually the same chords, same form, etc.—you still need to keep on your toes if you want to turn out an excellent performance, instead of a just satisfactory one. One aspect of this lies in thinking ahead, which is the subject of this lesson. In addition to avoiding getting tripped up by awkward positions/fingerings, it's crucial to building interesting lines that grow and expand with the song as necessary.

Anticipating Where You Want to Be to Minimize Shifts

Any time you branch out from the tried-and-true patterns, you run the risk of not landing on your feet if you're not careful. So try to make it a habit of looking ahead on beat 3 or so (a full measure for really fast tempos) if you're planning on moving into a different octave or significantly changing your pattern.

For example, let's say you're playing a standard boogie line in C out of seventh position, like this…

…and you want to move down to the lower register with a 1–♭7–6–5 pattern for measures 3–4 so you can lead smoothly to the low F note for the IV chord. If you play the C note on beat 1 of measure 3 at the same spot (fret 8, string 4), then you're going to have at least two shifts—or one really long, awkward one—to make it down to the F note. But, if you just think ahead a bit, you can shift down to the C note at fret 3, string 3 with your pinky, putting you in perfect position.

EXAMPLE 1

By the same token, if you want to shift up to the higher octave in measure 2, instead of fretting the C note on beat 1 of measure 2 with your pinky, take care of that with a single shift as well.

EXAMPLE 2

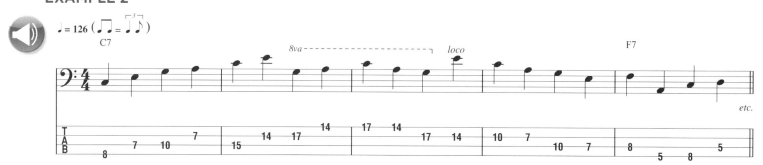

Anticipating a New Section

Many times, you'll be changing patterns with a new section (chorus, solo, etc.). For example, maybe you'll be moving from a walking line to a box pattern. If so, you can avoid an awkward shift if you think ahead.

Let's say you're in the key of A and ending one chorus with a walk up to the tonic on string 4. For the next section, you're going to be moving to the 1–8–♭7–5 box pattern. If you finish your walk-up by landing on the A with your pinky, you'll put yourself in a bind, because you'd have to move from there up two strings and two frets with your pinky in the space of an eighth note. We'll pick it up from measure 9 here:

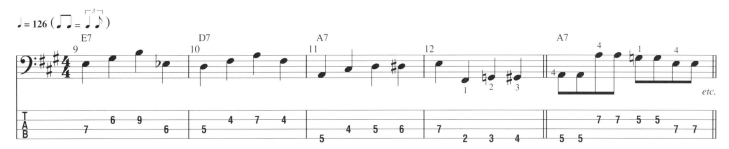

However, if you simply make the shift to the first finger on the downbeat of the new section, not only do you have a quarter note to make the shift, you're also putting yourself in perfect position for the new pattern.

EXAMPLE 3

Anticipating an Audible or Tag

Be sure to keep on the watch for audibles that may be called by the soloist or vocalist toward the end of the song. A very common one is the tag, which basically takes the form back to measure 9 (the V chord) for one more time through the ending before the *actual* ending. Once you get toward the end of the song, start watching/listening for this just in case.

EXAMPLE 4

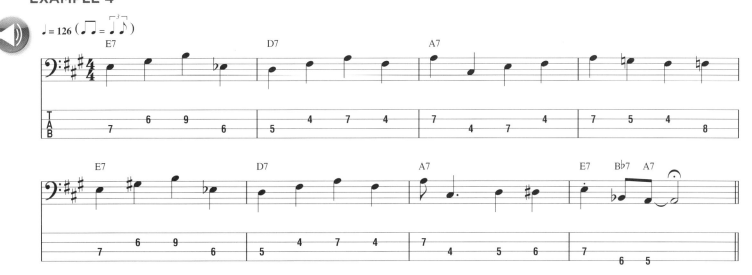

Summary

You can save yourself some awkward moments and produce a much smoother bass line with a bit of forethought. The more you do this, the more it will become habit, and you won't have to think ahead anymore! Imagine that!

LESSON #92: THAT PESKY 3RD

There are some blues tunes in which it's not entirely clear whether the tonality is dominant or minor. In those instances, it's very difficult to decide which 3rd—major or minor—to use. You don't want to ruin a mood by throwing a bright, happy major 3rd into things, but you don't want to possibly cause a clash by committing to a minor 3rd either. Whereas a blues guitarist or vocalist can bend their 3rds to all the cracks and crevices they desire, bassists are meant to provide a foundation for the sound. Therefore, it's generally not a good idea for the foundation to be "in the cracks" (there are exceptions, of course). In this lesson, we'll look at one of the most notorious trouble-maker chords in this regard and explore some of our options for navigating these somewhat treacherous waters.

The 7♯9 Chord

Ever since Hendrix, blues guitarists have enjoyed pulling out the 7♯9 chord, which sounds right in between a dominant chord and a minor chord. Here's a typical funk-blues groove that you might hear in A:

 A7♯9 GUITAR GROOVE

So what do we play under this? It's an altered dominant chord, so it does contain a major 3rd. But the ♯9th, which is enharmonic to the minor 3rd, is so prominent that it really lends a minor sound to the chord. Let's look at some options.

Option 1: Play the Major 3rd

Let's say you decide to be a stickler and insist on the major 3rd (C♯) because, after all, it *is* a dominant chord. Here's an example of how it might sound if you *really* commit to that major 3rd:

EXAMPLE 1

It's certainly a bold choice. Depending on context—including the vocal melody, contributions from horns or other instruments, etc.—it could work, but it might just be too happy-sounding. Here's how it would sound if you just hinted at the major 3rd:

EXAMPLE 2

Since the major 3rd is used more in passing, it's not quite as conspicuous. This is generally a safer choice if you don't have the luxury of working something out with the band beforehand.

Option 2: Play the Minor 3rd

You could also commit to the minor 3rd, which would be C natural. Just like the major 3rd, hanging on this note is risky, but it's usually a bit more acceptable in most circles. Here's how that might sound:

EXAMPLE 3

It kind of grinds a bit, but sometimes that's what you want in blues. The other option is to just use it in passing, which might sound like this:

EXAMPLE 4

This is probably the most common choice of all when dealing with a 3rd. It sounds tough and bluesy, but it stays out of the way of pretty much anything above it.

Option 3: Avoid the 3rd Altogether

If you can't get either one to sound right, you can simply avoid the 3rd altogether. In this case, you'd most likely construct the line using the root, 5th, and ♭7th. The 6th is sometimes an option as well. Here are two lines demonstrating this type of idea:

EXAMPLE 5

EXAMPLE 6

Summary

Ideally, you'd have a chance to rehearse with the band before performing the song and therefore could get input from the bandleader with regard to which sound he preferred. But, if you're thrown into the pit at an open mic or something, the strategies learned in this lesson can serve you well. When in doubt, play the 3rds staccato and don't dwell on them. When in *serious* doubt, just leave them out!

LESSON #93: TRANSCRIBE!

If you want to really expand your playing, there aren't many better methods than transcription. This can be a bass solo, a bass lick, or an entire song (highly recommended). It may sound counter-intuitive: how can you expand *your* playing by copying someone else? Won't you just end up sounding like them? That's a good question, but it only scratches the surface of the benefits of transcription. Let's examine this a bit more.

Identity Crisis

First of all, you're not going to be *copying* anyone; you're simply going to be expanding your vocabulary. No one lives in a bubble, and therefore everyone is influenced by multiple sources on a daily basis. If someone were to grow up alone, stranded on a desert island with nothing but an upright bass (a likely scenario), then they might develop a truly original bass style. (Then again, they might not.) Most players' styles are really just amalgamations of others that came before them. You don't have to do *everything* differently to be recognizable; you just have to do a few things, and this comes naturally.

Just as in the English language, we aren't copying someone if we use a few of the same words as they do. Now, some musicians may have a few signature phrases, and, just as you don't want to plagiarize some sentences or paragraphs from someone's magazine article, you don't want to play someone else's signature phrases. But sentences and paragraphs are made up of words, and that's the music equivalent of the type of vocabulary you'll be expanding. You'll be learning how to connect notes and phrases differently, how to use space differently, and how to create tension and release, etc.

It Does an Ear Good

Transcription is some of the best ear training that you can do. When you sit down with a recording and dissect it, top to bottom, you'll surely hear several things played several times. No bassist plays something new in every measure; they're going to have devices or lines that they fall back on. As a result, you'll begin to recognize them and start to make a connection between your ear (or mind) and your fingers. Just as you can listen to a word and know how to spell it without reading it on a page, you can learn to listen to a musical phrase and know how to play it without having to read it or hunt and peck for the notes. The more you do it, the better you'll be.

The (Musical) Universe Is Expanding

By listening closely to the bass lines from several different songs by several different artists, you're bound to notice other things as well, such as drum fills, guitar licks, piano comping, etc. This may be a completely subconscious thing, but you'll definitely be absorbing this stuff on some level. I can't count the number of times that I discovered another musician while transcribing a completely separate instrument. One will lead to another, and before you know it, you'll have discovered an entirely new galaxy of music.

Tools of the Trade

Some people, myself included, prefer to go old school with the process. By this I mean using a pencil and manuscript paper and handwriting everything. Others like to use notation software and transcribing programs, which allow you to slow down the audio while retaining the pitch and/or isolate different instruments for ease of identification. Both methods are valid, and it's really just a matter of preference. Here are several tools to keep at your disposal if you plan on spending a healthy amount of time transcribing:

- Pencils and sharpener
- Erasers
- Headphones
- Metronome
- Tuner
- Musical dictionary
- Desktop lamp (if your area is not well-lit)

Also make sure you have a comfortable chair to sit in and a desk that's a good height so you don't have to slouch. Be sure to take occasional breaks and walk around—five minutes out of every hour or 45 minutes is a good start—to give your ears a rest and to get the blood flowing!

Summary

Once you take the plunge and transcribe your first few bass lines, you'll no doubt begin to see the benefits. It's really kind of a miracle music drug, but it's perfectly legal and has no negative side effects. (You might miss your favorite TV show or something but, come on—you can record it and watch it later if you really need to.) And there is nothing that says you have to transcribe bass parts exclusively. In fact, if you really want to expand your horizons, try transcribing other instruments for bass some time. Good luck and enjoy.

It's hard to think of a more influential bass player in the blues realm than Willie Dixon. The man wasn't just a killer upright player, he also wrote many of the blues classics that we still play today. Among his many compositions are "Hoochie Coochie Man," "My Babe," "I Just Want to Make Love to You," "Little Red Rooster," and "Spoonful," to name just a few. It's no stretch to say that Dixon was one of the most influential post-war blues artists of all. Aside from being a proficient upright bassist, guitarist, vocalist, and songwriter, he also produced dozens of hits for the Chess and Cobra labels.

Equipment

Dixon got his start on a homemade "tin-can bass" and actually recorded some sessions with it from 1939 to the early '40s. Eventually, he moved on to the upright and settled on a King Moretone as his instrument of choice. He briefly dabbled with the Fender Precision when it came out in 1951, but he ended up giving it to a friend because he didn't play it much. Dixon claimed to have had only around five basses in his lifetime. In his later years, he played a Kay upright bass as well.

Modified Two-Feel

Willie had a cool way of working the two-feel, even in a slow-ish 12/8 blues, wandering in and out of it at times and/or using different notes than you might expect. For example, he might play the 5th on beat 1 and the root on beat 3. Here's an example of this kind of idea in D:

EXAMPLE 1

Walking

Dixon also had a very cool walking style. It was jazzy, but not the typical jazz walking style; instead, it was kind of a blues/jazz hybrid. He repeated notes at times and kept it fairly diatonic.

EXAMPLE 2

Blues Riffs

Then there were all those awesome song riffs that he created. Or, if he didn't create them, he situated them into classic songs with utter skill. Here are two of the most common:

EXAMPLE 3

EXAMPLE 4

Summary

Many people acknowledge Willie for his contributions without ever actually going back and listening to his music. That's a shame because he was an outstanding performer, as well as a writer. His bass playing was always groovin', even when he played some flashier stuff (and he could!). If you call yourself a blues fan, you owe it to yourself to not only acknowledge Dixon's contributions, but to listen to them as well!

LESSON #95: DONALD "DUCK" DUNN STYLE

Donald "Duck" Dunn's resumé speaks for itself. As a member of Booker T. & the M.G.'s, the Blues Brothers, and a regular session player for Stax records in the '60s and '70s, Dunn's playing graced hundreds of the biggest records of the day, including Aretha Franklin's "Respect," Wilson Pickett's "The Midnight Hour," Otis Redding's "Dock of the Bay" and "I've Been Loving You," Sam & Dave's "Hold On, I'm Coming," and Albert King's "Born Under a Bad Sign," to name but a few. He barely slowed up from the '80s onward, playing with Tom Petty, Eric Clapton, Muddy Waters, Freddie King, Rod Stewart, Bill Withers, Neil Young, and many others. He left us too soon, dying in 2012 at the age of 70.

Equipment

Like many of the day, the Memphis-born Dunn was a Fender Precision player. He owned the first one that he bought, a 1958 sunburst model, throughout his entire life, though he made use of several others throughout his career as well. Like James Jamerson, Dunn preferred La Bella flat-wounds for their feel and tone. In 1998, Fender produced a Duck Dunn signature model, and Lakland did the same in a 2005 with a bass highly modeled after the Fender Precision but with a Fender Jazz-like neck on it. After that, he played both Lakland and Fender basses for the remainder of his career.

In the Stax studio days, he recorded with an Ampeg B-15 almost exclusively. Though he experimented with a piggyback Fender Bassman model, he didn't like it and ended up giving it to a friend. For live shows, he's made use of Ampegs (SVT models), Kustoms (the "tuck-and-roll" model), and Gallien-Kruegers throughout the years.

Shuffles

Duck had a great shuffle feel and would mix standard and altered boogie lines with speedy triplet fills—all with a stellar feel, of course. His articulation was usually more on the staccato side with this type of thing, which gave his lines great punch and clarity.

EXAMPLE 1

Here's a typical Dunn example. It's a moderate shuffle in E.

Blues-Rock Riff Styles

As a member of Booker T. & the M.G.'s, Duck backed many artists for the Stax label throughout the years, laying down some serious grooves in the blues-rock style.

EXAMPLE 2

Here's a line reminiscent of his style, played in a straight-eighths groove in C♯ minor. Pay attention to the rests and staccato markings.

R&B Grooves

Duck wasn't afraid to stick his neck out and create his own hook to make the song that much more memorable. This includes playing in the upper register at times and almost acting as a counter-melody.

EXAMPLE 3

Here's an example of this idea in E major:

Summary

Whether he was backing Albert King, Freddie King, Eric Clapton, or even Joan Baez, Duck always sat deep in the pocket and never overplayed. His lines were toe-tapping, punchy, and filled with soul. To hear this for yourself, be sure to check out his work with Stax Records.

TOMMY SHANNON STYLE

During the 1980s, behind bandleader Stevie Ray Vaughan, Tommy Shannon helped create perhaps the greatest blues revival ever and, as a result, has gone on to become one of the most famous blues bassists around.

Since Vaughan's tragic death in 1990, Tommy has kept busy musically, playing with Doyle Bramhall II, Charlie Sexton, and Chris Layton in Arc Angels, and also forming Storyville with Layton, David Grissom (of John Mellencamp's band), Malford Milligan, and David Holt. He's also shared the stage with Eric Clapton, Susan Tedeschi, Kenny Wayne Shepherd, the Rolling Stones, Little Richard, Jonny Lang, Eric Johnson, and John Mayer, to name a few.

Equipment

Although Shannon does make use of the requisite Fender P-Bass, he actually tends to favor the Fender Jazz bass more frequently, his favorite being a white, battle-worn 1962 model with a red tortoise-shell pickguard. He uses both flat- and round-wound strings. Over the years, his other basses include a Music Man StingRay, Yamaha BB, and custom Foderas. During the Stevie Ray years, he usually played Peavey amps and cabinets (or Deitz cabs), although he occasionally made use of others. Since then, he's played an Ampeg SVT with Hartke cabs, Trace Elliot amps and cabs, as well as Eden. Remember that, during his time with Stevie Ray Vaughan, he tuned down a half step to match Stevie's guitar, so be sure to do that if you want to play along to any SRV recordings.

Slow Blues

Tommy's slow-blues feel was quite improvisatory; he rarely played the same thing twice and mixed it up quite a bit, both rhythm- and note-wise.

EXAMPLE 1

Here's a typical example of a line in G. Notice the numerous chromatic passing/leading tones and the interesting choices where he'll abandon an idea that you're expecting in favor of something else (as in measures 2 and 4).

Shuffle

Shannon got plenty of practice playing shuffles with Stevie Ray, and he developed a unique approach to them. When playing open keys, such as E, he would often pivot off the open strings on the bottom with a moving line on top.

EXAMPLE 2

R&B/Funk-Blues Feel

EXAMPLE 3

Here's an example in B that demonstrates Shannon's funkier side.

JACK BRUCE STYLE

Although the late, great Jack Bruce is mostly known to the music world as 1/3 of '60s supergroup Cream, his skillset extends far beyond playing blues rock. He's actually quite a skilled classical and jazz player as well. During the early to mid-'60s, Bruce met both of his future partners in Cream while playing in other bands—drummer Ginger Baker with Blues Incorporated, and Eric Clapton with John Mayall & the Bluesbreakers. After a brief stint with Manfred Mann, followed by an even shorter one with Clapton and Steve Winwood in Powerhouse, Bruce formed Cream with Baker and Clapton. The rest, as they say, is history.

Equipment

One of Bruce's first electric basses was actually the Fender Bass VI, which was a short-scale, six-string bass tuned just like a guitar, only an octave lower (and obviously featuring thicker string gauges). He used this bass to record most of *Fresh Cream*. After that, he moved on to the iconic Gibson EB-3—also a short-scale bass—for which he would become known in Cream. He briefly played some long-scale fretless basses by Aria and Spector in the late '70s before settling on Warwick, with whom he designed the Jack Bruce Signature Model, also a fretless. During the '60s, Bruce plugged into Marshall 100 heads with matching 4x12 cabinets. By cranking the volume, he produced the heavy, slightly overdriven sound that became so popular in Cream. In later years, he began using a Samson wireless unit and a Hartke 7000 head with four Hartke XL cabinets: two 4x10s and two 1x15s.

12-Bar Uptempo Blues Rock

On uptempo blues-rock tunes, Bruce would often use moveable box-shaped patterns and build lines from the root, octave, ♭7th, 5th, and (sometimes) the 4th of each chord. Here's an example of this idea in A. Note the staccato articulation that's mixed in with the sustained notes.

EXAMPLE 1

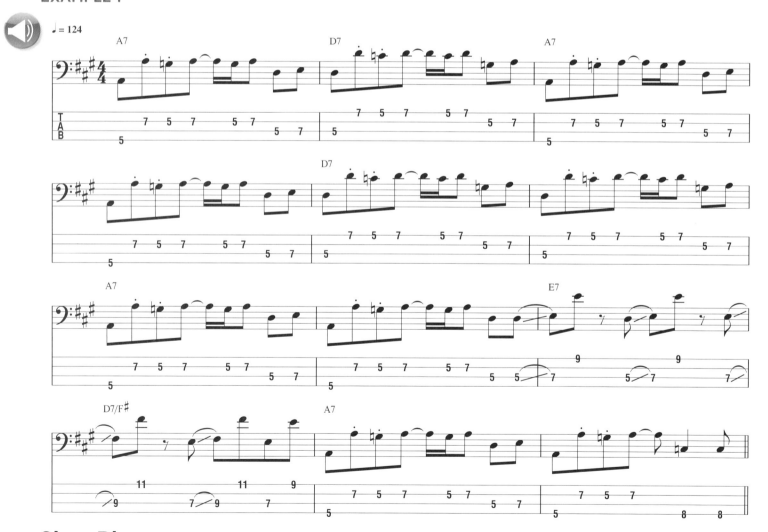

Slow Blues

When playing slow blues during the Cream days, Bruce mixed riffs—the kind you might find in a Willie Dixon-penned one-chord blues—into the 12-bar format in a way that the bass almost served as an independent hook in the song.

EXAMPLE 2

Riff Blues

Bruce would also make use of some colorful notes when creating riffs, which he often would then filter through the 12-bar format.

EXAMPLE 3

ROSCOE BECK STYLE

A firmly established session player and producer, Roscoe Beck is most widely known for his tenure with Robben Ford & the Blue Line—the trio that also featured Tom Brechtlein on drums. However, he's also performed with Eric Johnson and Leonard Cohen extensively, among numerous others, including Stevie Ray Vaughan, Jimmie Vaughan, and the Dixie Chicks, to name a few.

Equipment

Beck is mostly a Fender guy and has made use of several Jazz basses throughout his career. He collaborated with Fender to create four- and five-string Signature models in the mid-'90s. They featured a very elaborate electronics system, consisting of two humbucking pickups, three-position pickup selector, master volume and tone controls (with push/pull mid-shaping), and two mini-toggle switches, for extreme versatility. In the amp department, Beck has made extensive use of Trace Elliot amps and cabs throughout the years, including his time with Robben Ford. He's a prominent endorser of T.C. Electronic and has used a number of their products over the years. One of the most conspicuous is the 1210 chorus, which he uses when emulating an organ with his tapping technique.

Funky Blues Feel

Roscoe can funk with the best of them. He's got a full, rich tone and blends a sense of structure and improvisation in a masterful way. He'll usually anchor the line with a repetitive phrase but will keep it interesting with various fills in between.

EXAMPLE 1

Shuffle

Roscoe has an extensive background in jazz and other styles, which informs his blues playing quite a bit. In shuffles, he'll often choose to stick to mostly quarter notes for more of a traditional jazz/blues feel, but he won't always walk the line either.

EXAMPLE 2

Organ-Emulation Tapping Style

To achieve the organ tapping effect, Roscoe will hammer out a bass line on the bottom two strings with his fret-hand fingers while tapping dyads with his pluck hand on the top two strings.

EXAMPLE 3

Jerry "The Groovemaster" Jemmott began playing acoustic bass at age 10 but had made the move to electric by the time he was an early teenager. Based in New York, Jemmott was discovered by sax legend King Curtis at age 20, which led to a regular career as a session musician for Atlantic records. From the late '60s to the mid-'70s, Jemmott played on recordings by some of the biggest names in R&B and blues, including Ray Charles, Aretha Franklin, Roberta Flack, Wilson Pickett, B.B. King, Freddie King, Chuck Berry, Otis Rush, and Mike Bloomfield, to name a few.

He also worked with several jazz artists, including Herbie Hancock, Lionel Hampton, George Benson, and Eddie Harris, among others. By the late '70s, Jemmott had moved on to film and theater as an arranger and conductor. In the '80s, he was hand-picked by Jaco Pastorius to be the host for Jaco's instructional bass video, *Modern Electric Bass*.

Equipment

Jerry has been a long-time user of Fender Jazz basses, making use of dozens of different models throughout the years, but his favorites are a '65 and '69 model. Back in the day, he strung them with La Bella flats and usually played through an Ampeg B-15 or a Fender B/300 amp. Since then, he's made use of a custom Abe Rivera bass, a 1950 Kay upright, Ampeg SVT6 amp, and Fender Bassman 200 combo amp.

Minor Blues with a Straight-Eighths Feel

Jemmott can not only funk it up severely, he can also lay back and ride a fat groove with only the bare necessities. Here's an example of that kind of idea, played as a minor blues in B in which the same hypnotic rhythm is applied almost throughout, with the occasional pickup phrase used to connect the chords. The half-step leading tones lend a unique sound to the line.

EXAMPLE 1

Funk/R&B Feel

When it came to funk and R&B, it doesn't get any more in the pocket than Jerry. He could blend syncopated lines and dead notes into extremely catchy and musical-sounding bass lines.

EXAMPLE 2

Here's an example of this kind of thing over a funky one-chord groove in D. Notice the syncopated downbeat (the "uh" of beat 4) and the descending 5ths phrase in measures 3 and 7, which also syncopates the downbeat by placing the accent on the "and" of beat 1. The only time the downbeat is hit is in measures 1 and 5.

Slow Blues

With his spacious feel and expansive note choices, Jemmott can make a slow blues sound bigger than the Grand Canyon. To demonstrate, here's an example in the key of D. Take note of the use of space (lots of dotted half notes), the gentle syncopations (accenting beats 5 and 11 of the 12/8 meter) in measures 11–12, and the use of chromatic lines to transition between chords.

EXAMPLE 3

Summary

It's not difficult to throw a stone onto a pile of '60s soul records and hit one with Jemmott's bass playing on it. But be sure to check out his work with King Curtis, Aretha Franklin, B.B. King, Otis Rush, and Ray Charles. If you want to learn how to stay deep in the pocket while retaining the freedom to move about, you have to listen to Jerry. Others may do it differently, but no one does it better.

Chicago-born Johnny B. Gayden started playing bass at the ripe age of 12. He taught himself by playing along to his favorite recordings by bands like the Beatles, Wilson Pickett, the Rolling Stones, Muddy Waters, Howlin' Wolf, and James Brown. In 1973, after high school, he began touring with Son Seals, which began an extended collaboration that resulted in recording four albums with Son throughout the years. After briefly touring with the Staple Sisters in the mid-'70s, he got his big break in 1979, when he landed a gig with the "Iceman," Albert Collins. He recorded nine albums with Collins, including the Grammy-winning *Showdown* (with Johnny Copeland and Robert Cray). It's through Albert that most people became aware of Johnny's soulful, funky style.

Equipment

Currently, Gayden endorses GHT Strings, Washburn basses, and Eden amplifiers. He uses an Eden 800 World Tour model with several speaker cabs of varying configurations. His tone is definitely brighter than the typical blues tone, which is due to his use of round-wound strings and his amplifier settings. This helps it cut through the thick horns that were often featured in Albert Collins' music.

Funk-Blues Feel

Gayden's funk lines were often punchy and repetitive. He'd stick out of the mix pretty well due to his tone, which was much more pointed than the typical blues sound. He'd often take the same basic pattern and repeat it throughout the 12-bar form, transposing it for each chord.

EXAMPLE 1

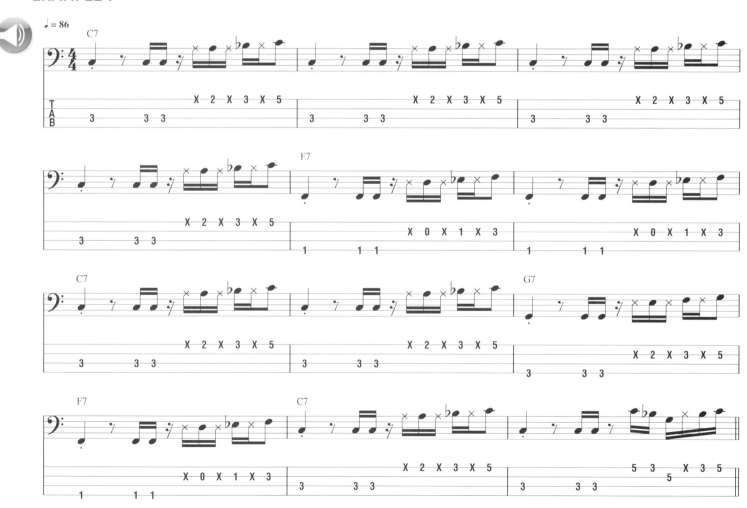

EXAMPLE 2

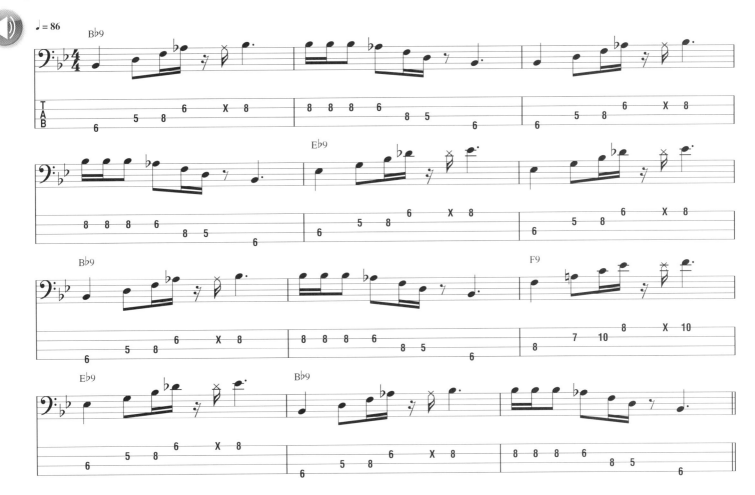

Shuffle

EXAMPLE 3

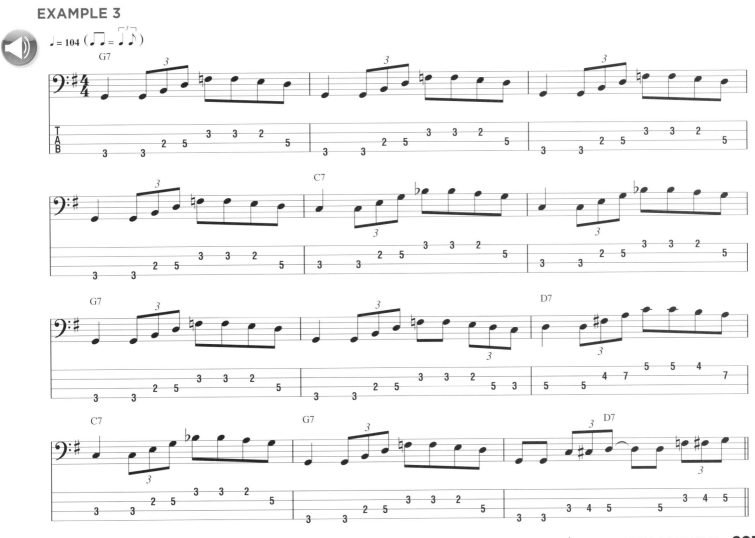

BASS RECORDED VERSIONS

Bass Recorded Versions feature authentic transcriptions written in standard notation and tablature for bass guitar. This series features complete bass lines from the classics to contemporary superstars.

25 All-Time Rock Bass Classics
00690445 / $14.95

25 Essential Rock Bass Classics
00690210 / $15.95

Avenged Sevenfold – Nightmare
00691054 / $19.99

Best of Victor Bailey
00690718 / $19.95

Bass Tab 1990-1999
00690400 / $16.95

Bass Tab 1999-2000
00690404 / $14.95

Bass Tab 2013
00121899 / $19.99

Bass Tab White Pages
00690508 / $29.99

The Beatles Bass Lines
00690170 / $14.95

The Beatles 1962-1966
00690556 / $18.99

The Beatles 1967-1970
00690557 / $19.99

The Best of Blink 182
00690549 / $18.95

Blues Bass Classics
00690291 / $14.95

Boston Bass Collection
00690935 / $19.95

The Best of Eric Clapton
00660187 / $19.95

Stanley Clarke Collection
00672307 / $19.95

Funk Bass Bible
00690744 / $19.95

Hard Rock Bass Bible
00690746 / $17.95

**Jimi Hendrix –
Are You Experienced?**
00690371 / $17.95

Incubus – Morning View
00690639 / $17.95

Iron Maiden Bass Anthology
00690867 / $22.99

Jazz Bass Classics
00102070 / $17.99

Best of Kiss for Bass
00690080 / $19.95

**Lynyrd Skynyrd –
All-Time Greatest Hits**
00690956 / $19.99

Bob Marley Bass Collection
00690568 / $19.95

Mastodon – Crack the Skye
00691007 / $19.99

Megadeth Bass Anthology
00691191 / $19.99

Metal Bass Tabs
00103358 / $19.99

Best of Marcus Miller
00690811 / $24.99

Motown Bass Classics
00690253 / $14.95

Muse Bass Tab Collection
00123275 / $19.99

Nirvana Bass Collection
00690066 / $19.95

No Doubt – Tragic Kingdom
00120112 / $22.95

The Offspring – Greatest Hits
00690809 / $17.95

**Jaco Pastorius –
Greatest Jazz Fusion Bass Player**
00690421 / $19.99

The Essential Jaco Pastorius
00690420 / $19.99

Pearl Jam – Ten
00694882 / $16.99

Pink Floyd – Dark Side of the Moon
00660172 / $14.95

The Best of Police
00660207 / $14.95

Pop/Rock Bass Bible
00690747 / $17.95

Queen – The Bass Collection
00690065 / $19.99

R&B Bass Bible
00690745 / $17.95

Rage Against the Machine
00690248 / $17.99

The Best of Red Hot Chili Peppers
00695285 / $24.95

**Red Hot Chili Peppers –
Blood Sugar Sex Magik**
00690064 / $19.95

Red Hot Chili Peppers – By the Way
00690585 / $19.95

**Red Hot Chili Peppers –
Californication**
00690390 / $19.95

**Red Hot Chili Peppers –
Greatest Hits**
00690675 / $18.95

**Red Hot Chili Peppers –
I'm with You**
00691167 / $22.99

**Red Hot Chili Peppers –
One Hot Minute**
00690091 / $18.95

**Red Hot Chili Peppers –
Stadium Arcadium**
00690853 / $24.95

**Red Hot Chili Peppers –
Stadium Arcadium: Deluxe Edition**
Book/2-CD Pack
00690863 / $39.95

Rock Bass Bible
00690446 / $19.95

Rolling Stones
00690256 / $16.95

**Stevie Ray Vaughan –
Lightnin' Blues 1983-1987**
00694778 / $19.95

Best of Yes
00103044 / $19.99

Best of ZZ Top for Bass
00691069 / $22.99

HAL•LEONARD®
CORPORATION
7777 W. BLUEMOUND RD. P.O. BOX 13819
MILWAUKEE, WISCONSIN 53213

Visit Hal Leonard Online at
www.halleonard.com

Hal Leonard BASS PLAY-ALONG

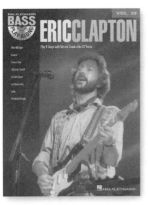

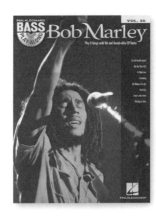

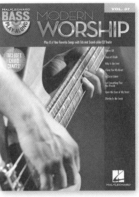

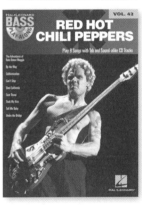

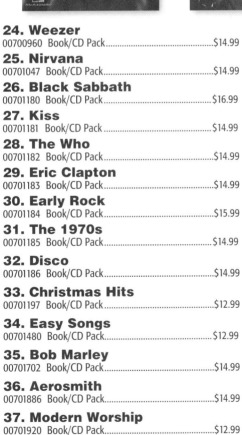

The Bass Play-Along™ Series will help you play your favorite songs quickly and easily! Just follow the tab, listen to the CD or online audio to hear how the bass should sound, and then play along using the separate backing tracks. The melody and lyrics are also included in the book in case you want to sing, or to simply help you follow along. The audio files are enhanced so you can adjust the recording to any tempo without changing pitch!

1. Rock
00699674 Book/CD Pack..$12.95

2. R&B
00699675 Book/CD Pack..$14.99

3. Pop/Rock
00699677 Book/CD Pack..$12.95

4. '90s Rock
00699679 Book/CD Pack..$12.95

5. Funk
00699680 Book/CD Pack..$12.95

6. Classic Rock
00699678 Book/CD Pack..$12.95

7. Hard Rock
00699676 Book/CD Pack..$14.95

9. Blues
00699817 Book/CD Pack..$14.99

10. Jimi Hendrix Smash Hits
00699815 Book/CD Pack..$17.99

11. Country
00699818 Book/CD Pack..$12.95

12. Punk Classics
00699814 Book/CD Pack..$12.99

13. Lennon & McCartney
00699816 Book/CD Pack..$14.99

14. Modern Rock
00699821 Book/CD Pack..$14.99

15. Mainstream Rock
00699822 Book/CD Pack..$14.99

16. '80s Metal
00699825 Book/CD Pack..$16.99

17. Pop Metal
00699826 Book/CD Pack..$14.99

18. Blues Rock
00699828 Book/CD Pack..$14.99

19. Steely Dan
00700203 Book/CD Pack..$16.99

20. The Police
00700270 Book/CD Pack..$14.99

21. Rock Band – Modern Rock
00700705 Book/CD Pack..$14.95

22. Rock Band – Classic Rock
00700706 Book/CD Pack..$14.95

23. Pink Floyd – Dark Side of The Moon
00700847 Book/CD Pack..$14.99

24. Weezer
00700960 Book/CD Pack..$14.99

25. Nirvana
00701047 Book/CD Pack..$14.99

26. Black Sabbath
00701180 Book/CD Pack..$16.99

27. Kiss
00701181 Book/CD Pack..$14.99

28. The Who
00701182 Book/CD Pack..$14.99

29. Eric Clapton
00701183 Book/CD Pack..$14.99

30. Early Rock
00701184 Book/CD Pack..$15.99

31. The 1970s
00701185 Book/CD Pack..$14.99

32. Disco
00701186 Book/CD Pack..$14.99

33. Christmas Hits
00701197 Book/CD Pack..$12.99

34. Easy Songs
00701480 Book/CD Pack..$12.99

35. Bob Marley
00701702 Book/CD Pack..$14.99

36. Aerosmith
00701886 Book/CD Pack..$14.99

37. Modern Worship
00701920 Book/CD Pack..$12.99

38. Avenged Sevenfold
00702386 Book/CD Pack..$16.99

40. AC/DC
14041594 Book/CD Pack..$16.99

41. U2
00702582 Book/CD Pack..$16.99

42. Red Hot Chili Peppers
00702991 Book/CD Pack..$19.99

43. Paul McCartney
00703079 Book/CD Pack..$17.99

44. Megadeth
00703080 Book/CD Pack..$16.99

45. Slipknot
00703201 Book/CD Pack..$16.99

46. Best Bass Lines Ever
00103359 Book/Online Audio................................$17.99

48. James Brown
00117421 Book/CD Pack..$16.99

49. Eagles
00119936 Book/CD Pack..$17.99

FOR MORE INFORMATION, SEE YOUR LOCAL MUSIC DEALER,
OR WRITE TO:

HAL•LEONARD® CORPORATION
7777 W. BLUEMOUND RD. P.O. BOX 13819 MILWAUKEE, WI 53213

Prices, contents, and availability subject to change without notice.

Visit Hal Leonard Online at **www.halleonard.com**

1114

BASS BUILDERS

A series of technique book/CD packages created for the purposeful building and development of your chops. Each volume is written by an expert in that particular technique. And with the inclusion of audio, the added dimension of hearing exactly how to play particular grooves and techniques make these truly like private lessons.

BASS AEROBICS *(INCLUDES TAB)*
by Jon Liebman
00696437 Book/CD Pack.................................. $19.99

**BASS FITNESS –
AN EXERCISING HANDBOOK** *(INCLUDES TAB)*
by Josquin des Prés
00660177 .... $10.99

BASS FOR BEGINNERS *(INCLUDES TAB)*
by Glenn Letsch
00695099 Book/CD Pack.................................. $19.95

BASS GROOVES *(INCLUDES TAB)*
by Jon Liebman
00696028 Book/CD Pack.................................. $19.99

BASS IMPROVISATION *(INCLUDES TAB)*
by Ed Friedland
00695164 Book/CD Pack.................................. $17.95

BLUES BASS *(INCLUDES TAB)*
by Jon Liebman
00695235 Book/CD Pack.................................. $19.95

BUILDING ROCK BASS LINES
by Ed Friedland
00695692 Book/CD Pack.................................. $17.95

BUILDING WALKING BASS LINES
by Ed Friedland
00695008 Book/CD Pack.................................. $19.99

**RON CARTER –
BUILDING JAZZ BASS LINES**
00841240 Book/CD Pack.................................. $19.95

DICTIONARY OF BASS GROOVES *(INCLUDES TAB)*
by Sean Malone
00695266 Book/CD Pack.................................. $14.95

EXPANDING WALKING BASS LINES
by Ed Friedland
00695026 Book/CD Pack.................................. $19.95

**FINGERBOARD HARMONY
FOR BASS**
by Gary Willis
00695043 Book/CD Pack.................................. $17.95

FUNK BASS *(INCLUDES TAB)*
by Jon Liebman
00699348 Book/CD Pack.................................. $19.99

FUNK/FUSION BASS *(INCLUDES TAB)*
by Jon Liebman
00696553 Book/CD Pack.................................. $19.95

HIP-HOP BASS *(INCLUDES TAB)*
by Josquin des Prés
00695589 Book/CD Pack.................................. $14.95

JAZZ BASS
by Ed Friedland
00695084 Book/CD Pack.................................. $17.95

**JERRY JEMMOTT –
BLUES AND RHYTHM &
BLUES BASS TECHNIQUE** *(INCLUDES TAB)*
00695176 Book/CD Pack.................................. $17.95

JUMP 'N' BLUES BASS *(INCLUDES TAB)*
by Keith Rosier
00695292 Book/CD Pack.................................. $16.95

**THE LOST ART OF
COUNTRY BASS** *(INCLUDES TAB)*
by Keith Rosier
00695107 Book/CD Pack.................................. $19.95

**PENTATONIC SCALES
FOR BASS** *(INCLUDES TAB)*
by Ed Friedland
00696224 Book/CD Pack.................................. $19.99

REGGAE BASS *(INCLUDES TAB)*
by Ed Friedland
00695163 Book/CD Pack.................................. $16.95

'70S FUNK & DISCO BASS *(INCLUDES TAB)*
by Josquin des Prés
00695614 Book/CD Pack.................................. $15.99

**SIMPLIFIED SIGHT-READING
FOR BASS** *(INCLUDES TAB)*
by Josquin des Prés
00695085 Book/CD Pack.................................. $17.95

6-STRING BASSICS *(INCLUDES TAB)*
by David Gross
00695221 Book/CD Pack.................................. $12.95

**WORLD BEAT GROOVES
FOR BASS** *(INCLUDES TAB)*
by Tony Cimorosi
00695335 Book/CD Pack.................................. $14.95

HAL•LEONARD® CORPORATION
7777 W. BLUEMOUND RD. P.O. BOX 13819 MILWAUKEE, WI 53213

Visit Hal Leonard Online at **www.halleonard.com**

Prices, contents and availability subject to change without notice; All prices are listed in U.S. funds

0514

HAL·LEONARD BLUES PLAY-ALONG

For use with all the C, B♭, Bass Clef and E♭ Instruments, the Hal Leonard Blues Play-Along Series is the ultimate jamming tool for all blues musicians.

With easy-to-read lead sheets, and other split-track choices on the included CD, these first-of-a-kind packages will bring your local blues jam right into your house! Each song on the CD includes two tracks: a full stereo mix, and a split track mix with removable guitar, bass, piano, and harp parts. The CD is playable on any CD player, and is also enhanced so Mac and PC users can adjust the recording to any tempo without changing the pitch!

1. Chicago Blues
All Your Love (I Miss Loving) • Easy Baby • I Ain't Got You • I'm Your Hoochie Coochie Man • Killing Floor • Mary Had a Little Lamb • Messin' with the Kid • Sweet Home Chicago.
00843106 Book/CD Pack $12.99

2. Texas Blues
Hide Away • If You Love Me Like You Say • Mojo Hand • Okie Dokie Stomp • Pride and Joy • Reconsider Baby • T-Bone Shuffle • The Things That I Used to Do.
00843107 Book/CD Pack $12.99

3. Slow Blues
Don't Throw Your Love on Me So Strong • Five Long Years • I Can't Quit You Baby • I Just Want to Make Love to You • The Sky Is Crying • (They Call It) Stormy Monday (Stormy Monday Blues) • Sweet Little Angel • Texas Flood.
00843108 Book/CD Pack $12.99

4. Shuffle Blues
Beautician Blues • Bright Lights, Big City • Further on up the Road • I'm Tore Down • Juke • Let Me Love You Baby • Look at Little Sister • Rock Me Baby.
00843171 Book/CD Pack $12.99

5. B.B. King
Everyday I Have the Blues • It's My Own Fault Darlin' • Just Like a Woman • Please Accept My Love • Sweet Sixteen • The Thrill Is Gone • Why I Sing the Blues • You Upset Me Baby.
00843172 Book/CD Pack $14.99

6. Jazz Blues
Birk's Works • Blues in the Closet • Cousin Mary • Freddie Freeloader • Now's the Time • Tenor Madness • Things Ain't What They Used to Be • Turnaround.
00843175 Book/CD Pack $12.99

7. Howlin' Wolf
Built for Comfort • Forty-Four • How Many More Years • Killing Floor • Moanin' at Midnight • Shake for Me • Sitting on Top of the World • Smokestack Lightning.
00843176 Book/CD Pack $12.99

8. Blues Classics
Baby, Please Don't Go • Boom Boom • Born Under a Bad Sign • Dust My Broom • How Long, How Long Blues • I Ain't Superstitious • It Hurts Me Too • My Babe.
00843177 Book/CD Pack $12.99

9. Albert Collins
Brick • Collins' Mix • Don't Lose Your Cool • Frost Bite • Frosty • I Ain't Drunk • Master Charge • Trash Talkin'.
00843178 Book/CD Pack $12.99

10. Uptempo Blues
Cross Road Blues (Crossroads) • Give Me Back My Wig • Got My Mo Jo Working • The House Is Rockin' • Paying the Cost to Be the Boss • Rollin' and Tumblin' • Turn on Your Love Light • You Can't Judge a Book by the Cover.
00843179 Book/CD Pack $12.99

11. Christmas Blues
Back Door Santa • Blue Christmas • Dig That Crazy Santa Claus • Merry Christmas, Baby • Please Come Home for Christmas • Santa Baby • Soulful Christmas.
00843203 Book/CD Pack $12.99

12. Jimmy Reed
Ain't That Lovin' You Baby • Baby, What You Want Me to Do • Big Boss Man • Bright Lights, Big City • Going to New York • Honest I Do • You Don't Have to Go • You Got Me Dizzy.
00843204 Book/CD Pack $12.99

FOR MORE INFORMATION, SEE YOUR LOCAL MUSIC DEALER, OR WRITE TO:

HAL·LEONARD® CORPORATION
7777 W. BLUEMOUND RD. P.O. BOX 13819 MILWAUKEE, WI 53213